Asset Management

decision-making:

The SALVO Process

John Woodhouse MA FIAM MSaRS

Published by The Woodhouse Partnership Ltd, Prince Henry House, Kingsclere Business Park, Hampshire RG20 4SW, United Kingdom

For more information visit www.SALVOproject.org

First published 2014

ISBN 978-0-9563934-7-0

CONTENTS

Acknowledgements

This guidebook is a summary of the work of some very dedicated and smart people in several organisations, who have collaborated over a 4-year period to research, develop, document and test an integrated approach to better decision-making in asset management.

Many people have been involved in this initiative, either as members of active working parties or in peer review or field trials and rollout-programmes. However it is with great gratitude that the author wishes to acknowledge in particular the contributions of:

Alex Thomson, Andy Hunt, Jack Huggett, Peter Jay and Mike Dixon of TWPL, Richard Moore and Marc Sims of London Underground, Christine Pretorius of Sasol Synfuels, Karen Whitehall of Scottish Water, Phil Summerfield, Dr Meirion Morgan and Robert Lange of DSTL, Dr Ajith Parlikad of Cambridge University and Michelle le Blanc and Derrick Dunkley of National Grid.

Many thanks also go to Julie Fowler at TWPL for her constant and cheerful support to the whole programme.

1 Introduction

Good decision-making is at the very core of successful asset management. And, in line with the ISO Standard definition[1] of asset management as the *realisation of value from assets*, good decisions are those which deliver the greatest value over the whole asset life cycle. But this means that we need a clear understanding of what different people see as 'value', and how different types of value pull us in different directions. Business investors, for example, seek a combination of maximum financial return and acceptable levels of risk or security for their investment. Customers want high service levels or product quality, at lowest possible cost. Employees may regard working conditions, pay and job satisfaction as their priorities, while industry regulators, local society and other interest groups will have safety, environmental, social impact or other concerns.

So 'value' varies greatly in the eyes of the beholder and, since many of these interests compete, it is difficult to determine which asset management actions will achieve the best mix of satisfied stakeholders. This is why asset management decision-making is so critical and needs to be addressed carefully. If we get it right, there are very big benefits available (up to 30% of total asset life cycle costs can be eliminated, while simultaneously delivering and sustaining higher performance, reliability and safety). If we get it wrong, the spiral of high costs, poor performance, short-termism and dissatisfaction can destroy an organisation.

This guidebook explains what it takes to make the right decisions in the management of assets; not just in the steps and disciplines required, but also how to create a clear 'business case' to justify and communicate the outcomes, so that everyone can agree on **what** is worth doing, **when** and **why**.

Such decisions can rarely be made within discrete departments or by individuals without consultation and collaboration with others. Decisions require compromise between the disciplines and competing interests, so negotiation and trade-offs are necessary to achieve an 'optimal' solution.

---

[1] Ref. ISO55000 standard for asset management

This guidebook describes how to identify the competing factors, quantify their significance and identify the best value option. It addresses the difficulties of quantifying risk, coping with uncertain data or assumptions, exploring short-term and long-term consequences, and taking account of 'intangibles' within the decision-making process.

There are also many confusing techniques and methodologies that are described as 'decision support tools'. This guide summarises the common ones, their strengths and weaknesses, and where they fit into a more systematic approach to asset management decision-making. In particular it highlights the need for a *mixed toolbox* approach, since no single technique is capable of resolving all the many types of decision in the wide range of decision environments.

1.1   Scope and applicability

SALVO (*Strategic Assets: Lifecycle Value Optimization*) comprises a set of robust processes for evaluating and combining decisions associated with the life cycle management of assets. It also introduces a set of innovative decision support tools to focus on the right questions and explore options in terms of quantified business impact. The combination of processes and tools are suitable for any organisation, whether in the public or private sector, that is dependent on physical assets to deliver organisational objectives, and faces competing priorities and stakeholder expectations. SALVO processes and tools are also extremely well suited to satisfy the decision-making criteria required by the ISO 55001 standard for asset management.

SALVO enables the evaluation and optimization of both *individual* decisions (about discrete interventions on specific assets) and for *combinations* of activities across complex asset systems and networks. The processes also provide a full audit record of the basis for asset management decisions, including the impact of both financial and non-financial consequences. It is consistent with good practice risk management and financial control requirements.

The SALVO processes, tools and guidance have been developed by a consortium of organisations that manage a wide variety of asset types in different industry sectors and operating environments. The methods have very wide and flexible application, covering asset management decisions in all stages of the asset life cycle, with all sorts of stakeholder interests and organisational objectives. The processes are people-centric and specifically consider the challenges of making decisions based on realistic information availabilities which are often incomplete and uncertain. In summary they will help you to:

a) **Identify** and **prioritize** the most urgent issues for attention,
b) **Select** appropriate interventions, including 'non-asset' options,
c) **Evaluate** such options in terms of costs, benefits and risk impact,
d) **Optimize** their timings and frequencies,
e) **Integrate** individual activities into fully **optimized asset management strategies**.

1.2 Structure of this guidebook

This book provides a summary of the concepts and methods associated with optimized decision-making (sections 2 & 3), followed by a step-by-step explanation and illustration of the SALVO processes that apply to different decision types (sections 4 & 5). There is also a high level summary of the SALVO process and steps, provided as a foldout flap in the back cover of this book. This is also available as a large scale wall poster.

Much more detailed process maps, guidance, examples and practical tips are provided in the 'SALVO Technical Playbook', which is issued under commercial license with the DST software tools and 3-tier process training courses. Licensing arrangements range from discrete individuals to corporate systematic implementations, and certified consultant/facilitator options for those wishing to provide services that incorporate the SALVO processes and tools.

2 Decisions in asset management

Different asset life cycle stages represent very different decision-making environments and offer different opportunities to influence the whole life cycle value. In particular there are three distinct environments (see Figure 1).

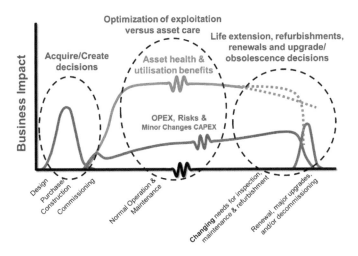

Figure 1. Different decision-making environments in asset life cycles

a) **Beginning of life stage:** in the 'green field' environment of initial investment, procurement or asset creation decisions, we have to make very significant choices with immediate and future cost implications and, potentially, long term business-critical consequences. But we have to make the decisions with inherently weak data, since we have no direct experience of the assets yet; our decisions are based upon potentially long-term forecasts and assumptions about demand, economics, supply chains and resources. So we are facing high cost, business-critical decisions with uncertain information, and the whole asset life cycle in which to suffer the consequences of our misjudgements.

Furthermore, we tend to compound these decision-making problems with the bad habit of recognising and rewarding engineering or construction projects based mainly on the easiest short-term things to measure, such as delivery 'on-time and under-budget'. This means that subsequent operability, reliability, maintainability and sustainability are treated as less significant in decision-making.

As often quoted in life cycle costing papers and training materials, 80% of the whole life cycle cost may be pre-determined during the design stage, yet only 20% of the cost is actually incurred during the beginning-of-life phase. But, whether we are buying an inkjet printer or a multi-million dollar turbo-compressor, building production facilities or hospitals, the pressure to reduce the initial purchase (or construction) cost is immediate and tangible, whereas future operating, maintenance and eventual renewal costs are fuzzy and, in many cases, 'someone else's problem'. We usually end up paying for it later, however.

b) The normal, 'steady-state' **operational stage** of an asset's life, involves the competing desires to *exploit the assets* to the maximum, while also needing to *care for them* to ensure ongoing usefulness. This creates a natural tension between exploiters (operations) and carers (maintenance) that must be addressed in the day-to-day decision-making. For example, shutting down a system for maintenance clearly impacts operations, and the way in which assets are operated or used can have a big effect upon their need for maintenance. Furthermore, there is often a time-lag to consider: decisions about what to do in the short term (operations and/or maintenance) often have a delayed effect upon the need for other actions later. Sweating the assets now, to achieve higher short-term performance, may result in performance losses (asset failures) and extra maintenance or earlier renewal costs in the future.

In contrast to the 'greenfield' decision-making, the operational phase gives us a chance to observe and capture real evidence about asset performance, condition, costs etc. So hard data can increasingly support the decision-making processes.

c) No matter how well assets are maintained, there can come a point where 'steady state' is no longer an option. This marks the **end-of-life** decision-making environment, where considerations of major investment such as renewal, modification or decommissioning must be considered (along with options to avoid or defer such interventions).

Of course, this 'aging assets' circumstance is not limited to cases of 'old' assets or deterioration of assets – it also includes changing *external* factors such as customer demand, technology overtake (obsolescence), competition, economics or supply chain changes. And, like the beginning-of-life phase, the 'brown field' redevelopment options represent potentially big costs, uncertainties and business consequences.

In contrast with the green field (beginning of life) cases, we do now have better knowledge and experience of the behaviour of the *current* assets. Nevertheless, extrapolations into the future will still be uncertain and there may be a variety of life extension options, renewal, upgrade or decommissioning issues to consider, many of which will involve high costs and uncertain future impacts.

And the *timing* of such interventions is often critical. When operating costs, performance or risks are changing (i.e. no longer in steady state), then the cost/benefit of refurbishment, replacement or modification (or contingency planning options such as purchase of spares while we can) are tightly dependent on the 'when?' decision. Decisions about aging assets are both business-critical and timing-critical.

2.1 Challenges we face in making good decisions

Before we introduce the methods for making these different decisions at different life cycle stages, we must first recognise the real-world problems that we face in making the objectively correct or best value choices. These practical problems are typical and widespread, so it is no use introducing sophisticated methods that will fail due to inadequate data, organisational constraints, workforce acceptance or competency. Our decision-making processes and tools must be able to cope with the following:

- **Conflicting interests** – if we only see the world from the perspective of a personal or departmental performance goal or budget responsibility, it will be hard to find and demonstrate the best value position for the organisation. Asset management decisions are invariably cross-disciplinary, so consultation, team-working and collaboration mechanisms are needed to get the right decisions made. Unfortunately we often encounter budget protectionism, vested interests and, even at senior management levels, a difference between what is *said* and what is *done or encouraged*.

- **Conflicting Performance Measures** – badly chosen performance indicators (KPIs) compound and reinforce the problem of functional silos. If one group can only succeed at the expense of another, then the search for best overall value can easily be lost in the noise of competing priorities and protectionism.

- **Short-termism** – hard evidence today (costs, asset performance) often carries more decision weight and credibility than future forecasts and probabilities. And this problem is compounded by management rotations, regulatory and political cycles (with each leader wishing to make a visible, tangible difference within their short period of responsibility). So decision-making methods will have to compensate; providing quantified and credible evaluation of future impacts when making decisions about immediate actions or expenditures.

- **Fire-fighting** behaviour can be a cultural habit that is hard to break. The reactive workload may be too great to allow 'time to think', or it may be just simpler to wait until forced to act. In such an environment, the shift to proactive, preventive and defect elimination activities is a big culture change. And we often make this worse by celebrating and rewarding the 'heroes' who cope well in an emergency – while failing to recognise and applaud those who do not have such crises in the first place.

- **Efficiency versus effectiveness** – for many years organisations have been chasing ever greater efficiency: doing what we do quicker, smarter, better, cheaper. Unfortunately this preoccupation with improving efficiency can sometimes result in "doing the *wrong* work 10% quicker/better/cheaper". Our decision-making methods need to ensure that we are *doing the right things* as well as *doing them right*.

- **Business and communications skills for engineers** – technical staff do not easily speak the same language as the finance director, and technical 'justifications' for asset improvements sometimes get rejected, even if they are the correct things to do. So it is not enough just to determine the right solution; the conclusion must be explained in business terms (value for money). And it is not only the financial approvers who will need convincing. Those who will be responsible for implementing the decision also need to understand and accept *why* it is the right decision. So explain-ability of the results will be a key feature of good asset management decision-making.

- **Quantification of risks** – nearly all asset management decisions will involve risks and uncertainties. So we need a rational and consistent management process for the wide range of commercial, technical, safety and customer/public perception risks that will be encountered. Furthermore, in the case of asset interventions such as inspections, maintenance and renewal, it is often the patterns of *changing* risks that matter most. Decision-making must consider risks that might be *introduced* by an intervention as well as the degradation-related, increasing risks that are perhaps the reason for considering an intervention in the first place.

- **Data** – too much of it, not enough of it, inadequate quality or the wrong sort, and how is it, or should it be, used? The whole subject of data, information and knowledge management is a mess for many organisations. And some very expensive mistakes are made in the over-ambition and under-delivery of 'solutions' to the problem: in many cases, the "Enterprise Asset (information) Management" (EAM) system has become a tail that is wagging the dog. So, whilst it is clear that 'fact-based' decisions are highly desirable, the identification of *what* data to collect, at what cost and time investment, and *how we would use it correctly*, must be part of pragmatic decision-making.

All of these issues have to be addressed in decision-making mechanisms that determine the right things to do, for the right reasons, at the right time. So the SALVO process has to be a very people-oriented, be able to cope with widely varying data quality, navigate conflicting agendas and yet still retain sufficient transparency so that conclusions are easily explainable to different audiences. Quite a challenge!

2.2 Two underlying sources of decision error

The SALVO project identified two primary ways in which a decision might be distorted or incorrect. These represent two[2] sources of error, and a decision can be wrong, or inaccurate, due to either or both of these reasons.

a) Errors in the information used (**'input' error**). This covers data quality issues and uncertainties created by data unavailability, biased or distorted sources and the use of extrapolations, forecasts and assumptions.

b) Errors in the interpretation and usage of the information (**'processing' error**). This incorporates the misinterpretation, subjective judgement, incorrect weighting of the factors involved, 'political' distortions and other human factors, as well as the simple lack of understanding in how to evaluate options correctly in terms of value and total asset life cycle impact.

---

[2] There is actually a 3rd source of error, found in the possible *misinterpretation of results*, but we consider and address this separately, through education and better ways of explaining conclusions.

Perhaps surprisingly, these two sources of error are largely independent. We could have fairly good information, yet misinterpret it and come to the wrong decision, or we can suffer from very poor quality data but manage to avoid compounding this further if we handle it carefully and correctly. Of course the 'double whammy' of poor data AND subjective, inconsistent interpretation will result in a lot of bad decisions (see Figure 2). Ideally, of course, we would make decisions on good quality data (whatever that means - we shall explore this next) and a rigorous, consistent evaluation of the implications to identify and select the best value option (we will have to consider what this means too).

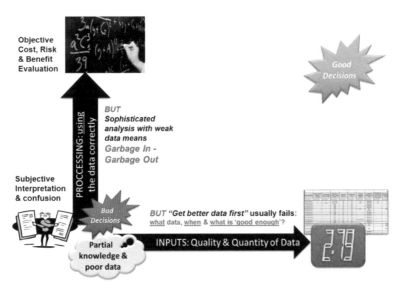

Figure 2. The twin challenges of data quality and correct usage.

Note: attempts to address either of these sources of decision error *on their own* usually fail. Let us now consider why:

2.2.1   Addressing the data problem first

Very commonly, when recognising the poor state of data or available information, the natural instinct of most people is to concentrate on 'getting better data first'. The thinking (often unstated) is that, once better data is available, we can start to consider what to do with it. Unfortunately this approach also yields many expensive mistakes.

Firstly, how can we say what data is worth collecting if we do not know how it would be used?   And, even if we manage to assemble an appropriate wish-list, *how much is worth spending*, and for *how long*, to achieve *what levels of data improvement?*   And *what constitutes 'good enough' data anyway?*

There are many, many experiences of collecting data that proved not to be appropriate or that was subsequently not used. There are also some extremely expensive examples of data improvement initiatives, based on well-intentioned principles and 'data standards', that simply could not be justified if a pragmatic cost-benefit test were applied to the efforts, timescales and subsequent usages.   Indeed, the idea that a generic standard of required data accuracy can be pre-determined and fulfilled is both naïve and counter-productive. It delays decisions, distracts priorities and is not achievable anyway.

So in determining what data improvements are actually worthwhile, we have to consider the potential impact and usage of the better quality information, and this in turn means we need to know, in advance, how the data should be used, and the 'cost' of not having it.

2.2.2   Doing lots of data analysis first

Another common mistake is to introduce sophisticated modelling and data analytics even when the available raw material (data) is uncertain but incomplete. Assumptions are used to fill the gaps and allow this approach to produce *apparently* impressive results (lots of tables and fancy graphics). But the conclusions often hide the compounding effects of many incorporated uncertainties.   This is why *"Garbage in = garbage out"* is often a truism.   Yet in organisations that have not yet learnt this lesson, an over-acceptance of output graphics and tables has even produced the cynical variant *"Garbage in, but Gospel out"*. Clearly we have to be very careful to faithfully represent uncertainty in inputs through to corresponding levels of uncertainty in the results.

We should be similarly sceptical of another 'black box' risk, commonly encountered when sophisticated analysis/modelling systems are introduced. In order to handle the information volume or complexity of required inputs, they need to make simplifications and incorporate embedded 'rules'. Such solutions are increasingly common as computing technology has developed so rapidly. Yet they often fail to provide transparency in the cause-effect relationships that must exist (and be seen to exist) between inputs/assumptions and outputs/decision implications. So, even if they do somehow generate the correct answers, they cannot easily explain or demonstrate *why* they are right. And, unless such credibility is established, acceptance of the decisions will continue to be a problem.

Note: these concerns are specifically directed at the use of overly sophisticated methods to the *evaluation and selection of optimal asset management strategies* (Step 4 in SALVO). In contrast, it is important to recognise that the initial identification and characterisation of problems is another large and fast-developing area of data analytics that has a very high value and success rate. Here the role of advanced systems is yielding very great improvements in early detection, in pattern-finding and in objective prioritization of improvement opportunities. As we will see, this is extremely valuable in Steps 1 and 2 of the SALVO process.

2.2.3   Iterative, step-wise approach

The SALVO approach concludes that a combined improvement approach to data and its usage is essential, involving an iterative, stepwise exploration (see Figure 3). Firstly we need to identify what information *might be* relevant, then using methods for capturing and quantifying it, even if only poor quality range-estimates are available. Next we have to test these estimates for their potential impact (sensitivity analysis) on the decision, thereby identifying *which data elements have the greatest effect*. This ensures that we focus any specific and more expensive data collection effort only on the elements that have a direct impact on the decision. In practice this is typically less than 10% of the potential factors involved in a decision. This process can iterate further, but not beyond the point where information is demonstrably adequate to make a robust and auditable decision.

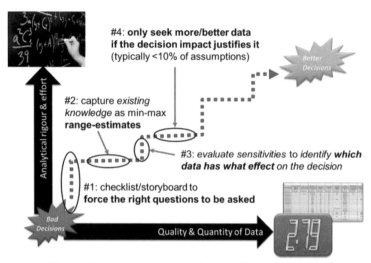

Figure 3. Step-wise approach to better decision-making

The SALVO process introduces the concept of 'Storyboards' to ensure that the right factors are considered and the right questions asked in each different type of decision. Such a structured approach, with a sequential consideration of the factors involved, greatly reduces the risk of 'jumping to conclusions' and overlooking a potentially significant influence on the decision. Forcing the right questions to be asked is a way of ensuring that the (inevitably) multi-disciplined inputs are all considered.

Revealed by these storyboards, many of the relevant questions will be difficult to answer with hard data or factual evidence, so the SALVO approach introduces a range-estimating and expert knowledge capture and quantification methods. These are used to create the first estimates that are sufficient for initial, exploratory 'what if?' explorations, to identify which assumptions have what impact or sensitivity. Targeted collection of only the decision-sensitive items is much more productive and resource-efficient. Furthermore, with proper calculations using such selectively focussed evidence, we can both make the right decision (e.g. when to replace an asset, or how many spares to hold) and demonstrate *why* this is the best solution.

2.3   Cost/risk/performance optimization principles

Most asset management decisions involve trade-off between competing objectives and stakeholder expectations. These business drivers are what defines 'value' for the organisation, and our goal is to find the best value mix of satisfying these needs. So the first priority must be to understand what the conflicting goals are, and how important they are. This, in itself, can be a challenge, since they are typically expressed in different forms, and their importance is not clear, quantified or consistent.

2.3.1   Rigour in considering factors involved

The European MACRO Project developed an elegant and comprehensive way to navigate the total picture, creating the generic 'Shamrock' diagram (see Figure 4). This shows how a wide range of apparent business drivers (outer ring) can be represented by just five quantification methods (inner group) for scaling the significance of the competing goals, and for resolving trade-offs and optimal compromises.

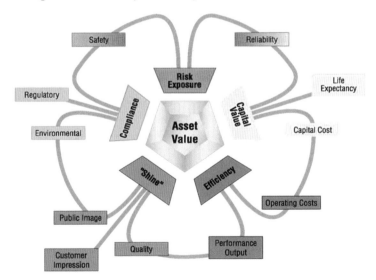

Figure 4. The Shamrock diagram[3] of competing organisational goals

---

[3] From European MACRO Project EU1488. See www.MACROproject.org

To test this approach for comprehensiveness or universal application, try answering the following question:

Does your organisation aim to be:
- *safe,*
- *reliable,*
- *sustainable (long lasting),*
- *cost efficient (both in capital investment and operating costs),*
- *high performing,*
- *delivering good quality services to satisfied clients,*
- *maintaining a good reputation,*
- *environmentally responsible and*
- *compliant with legal and regulatory requirements?*

This is simply a listing of all the items around the outside ring of the Shamrock – typical stakeholder interests and business objectives, which have very different symptoms of success, measurability and potential overlap or conflicting priority. The inner ring, however, represents the **only five methods available** for *quantifying their significance*. These five can be used to scale the significance of any combination of the outer ring goals, to resolve trade-off conflicts and find the optimal compromise (best value combination). And we know they can quantify *any* improvement opportunities because if there were zero risks, infinite asset life (full sustainability), 100% operational efficiency (including zero cost!), total compliance and 'happiness' (no intangible/perception problems and expectations always met), we would have perfection and there could be no scope for improvement.

The five core business drivers (the holy 'RELiCS') grouped into their methods of quantification and trade-off effects on asset value realisation are:

- **Risk** (any impacts that have discrete event impact and a probability or frequency of occurrence).
- **Efficiency** (the *ratio* between what we spend and what we achieve).

© The Woodhouse Partnership Ltd 2014

- **Life** expectancy (and the advantages of deferring capital expenditure).
- **Compliance** (the premium paid for compliance compared to what we would otherwise do).
- **Shine** (the premium paid for intangibles compared to what we would otherwise do).

The methods for quantifying the significance of these different factors vary widely. For example, we might be able to directly measure some aspects of efficiency (e.g. costs and performance output) but it is very hard to quantify the low probability/high consequence end of the risk spectrum. So, in addition to the selective use of any hard data that is available, we need to capture the knowledge and experience of those closest to the problem and their understanding of potential improvements or trade-off effects.

2.3.2 Collecting and using expert knowledge

The information required to perform a SALVO analysis can be summarised as follows:

1. The scope, direct and indirect **cost of the task/intervention** we are intending to evaluate (NB the cost may vary, or depend on condition found, so it may represent a *pattern* rather than just a simple 'cost per occasion').

2. The **relevant RELiCS** or dimensions of the Shamrock diagram that are involved in the decision. By focussing only on the factors involved in a particular decision it is easier to avoid distractions and considering data that is not relevant or needed.

3. For each decision-relevant factor, the **effects of the planned task** and the **task timing**/interval. This will almost always involve describing and quantifying a *pattern* e.g. a failure probability pattern, including risks introduced by the task, risks independent of the task timing, and risks that can be predicted, prevented, corrected or mitigated by the task.

Quantification of the different decision factors (Shamrock elements) can be difficult, particularly if they are interconnected and interdependent. This is where the SALVO Storyboards come in – for any decision type they provide the navigational discipline, and data capture formats to build a comprehensive picture, including the 'trade-offs', trends and patterns that often exist. The methods that are incorporated include careful consideration of human psychology as well as the mathematical rigour of correct treatment of complexities such as risk patterns that affect each other (for example, the survival profile from a failure mode changing the exposure to different failure mode).

Further to the software-supported Storyboards, there are also some human factors 'tips', discovered and/or developed by the SALVO Project, that are very valuable in the quantification stage. They can also be effective 'ice breakers' to initiate and focus a constructive discussion:

- **Higher than... Lower than**: the facilitator makes a suggestion to stimulate a response from the subject matter 'experts' to explore whether the reality is higher or lower than the proposal. This method is a well-established improvement over a simple "what if...?" question. The human brain finds it easier to make comparative estimates than it does to originate a spot estimate.

- **Range estimation:** Better still is the capture of a range-estimate directly; asking for min/max or earliest/latest extremes enables the 'expert' to qualify their contribution while also expressing their uncertainty. It can remove much of the reluctance to offer information (sometimes due to previous experiences of providing direct 'estimates' that were then misused/misinterpreted as being 'accurate'). DST software is equipped with extensive facilities for range-estimating, and performs automatic sensitivity analysis across the resulting combinations of uncertain data.

- **'Sherlock Holmes' method**: *"when you have eliminated the impossible, whatever remains ... must include the truth"*. If range-estimating is also proving difficult, then the questioning should focus initially on *incredible extremes,* yielding an easy rejection: *'of course not!'*). Then we shift a series of *'could it be as much/little as...?'* questions step-by-step towards the 'possible' area, and watching body language for the 'tipping point' where comfortable rejection ('definitely not') becomes a nervous 'maybe'. Coming in from both directions of easily-rejected extremes, we can find the boundaries zones of credibility – in other words a range-estimate!

For example, if trying to estimate something difficult, such as the frequency of a rare event, we start with an absurd suggested value, such as 'five times per day'. This will trigger an easy rejection (*"No way!"*) and we know that we are in the zone of the 'impossible'. By progressively changing this suggested value to, say, once per month, once per year, once per three years or once per 10 years, we can watch for the point where confident dismissal becomes a shrug of the shoulders, a pause, or an *"I don't know – maybe"* answer. This identifies the upper boundary or pessimistic limit of credibility. By then doing the same thing from the other direction (starting with examples from the incredible area of low probability), we can establish the other transition point of incredible/conceivable values. In other words we have moved the expert from a typical statement of *"I don't have a clue"* to a constructive, quantified range-estimate that encompasses the full range of his/her uncertainty and 'must include the truth'.

- **Premium paid for**.... is a further version of the Higher than/Lower than technique, that uses the Sherlock Holmes method to quantify, indirectly, the value of really intangible stuff. It is useful for putting a significance on Shine factors such as reputation, image, customer satisfaction or employee morale. Rather than estimate the positive value of success in these case, it can sometimes be easier to put a value on *not suffering the alternative*. In other words, quantify the amount we would be prepared to pay, or be paid, to compensate for *losing* the Shine (or suffering the 'tarnish'!). For example, if you were offered just $10 to have toothache, or incur some bad publicity in the local newspaper, would you accept the pain in return for the money being offered? What about $10,000? Or $100,000? Or $1 million....? At some point the 'premium paid for loss of Shine' becomes worth considering, and we have inferred a finite positive value of such intangibles. Clearly this also needs to be bracketed into range-estimates to reflect the uncertainty, the different perspectives and the volatility of such Shine factors.

Range-estimating and iterative, 'what if?' studies are key to the SALVO success. It takes seconds to try out an assumption and see if it has any effect upon the decision. So you should encourage speculation and experiment. This is a rapid way of a) learning about the decision drivers and b) identifying which areas you should spend more time and effort in obtaining greater information detail and accuracy. If you have conflicting opinions in the study team, for example, try the different values or ranges being proposed – it will soon be clear whether or not it is even worth having the debate about what the correct values should be (and if the information *does* prove to be decision-influencing, you can now demonstrate that it is worth some additional investigation effort).

When collecting 'tacit' knowledge from subject matter experts, you cannot do better than ensuring the following four-point checklist is adhered-to (Figure 5):

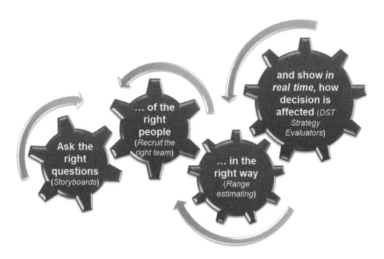

Figure 5. Rigour in obtaining expert knowledge

2.3.3   Optimization

'Optimized' is a much over-used, and often misused word. Yet it is the correct term for the best value compromise between competing objectives – which is what asset management decisions seek to deliver. And it is a very different place to the *localised, individual* interests such as 'minimum cost', 'minimum risk' or 'maximum performance'. It also should not be confused with the language or concept of a 'balance' point, as balancing seeks a point of *equality*, where component factors simply have the same significance. But **equality (balance) is not the goal** (see Figure 6). The <u>optimum</u> is the point where the total value (sum) of all costs, risks, performance losses etc. is at its lowest combined 'cost' to the business. In SALVO language we call this the lowest Total Business Impact.

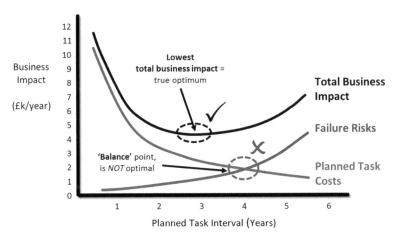

Figure 6. Example of conflicting factors and true meaning of 'optimum'

2.3.3.1 Optimizing with uncertain data

A common concern with any quantitative technique and decision optimization is the lack of quality data. Section 2.3.2 discussed this in detail, and how SALVO processes help at least to establish initial range-estimates. In the optimization stage, these range-estimates enable sensitivity-testing to identify the impact of data uncertainty. By very rapid 'what if?' calculations, we can explore the extremes of all uncertain inputs, revealing the effect upon our decision. Not only does this show whether or not the data quality should be a genuine concern, but it also reveals the optimistic/pessimistic limits for the decision itself – for example the maximum range for the optimal timing of asset replacement (see Figure 7).

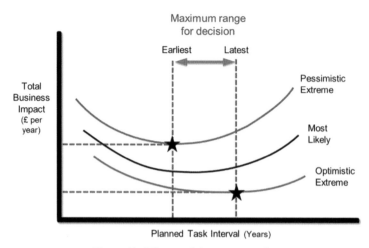

Figure 7. Effects of data uncertainty

SALVO takes this one step further still. If there is uncertainty in the *result*, due to the data weaknesses, then software can calculate and recommend the strategy that is *least vulnerable to such uncertainty* (see Figure 8). In other words, the intervention timing that, if it proves wrong due to the data error, will incur the smallest cost of such error. Furthermore, it can calculate what this vulnerability is worth in financial terms. This corresponds to a 'cost of uncertainty' and also represents the *maximum benefit possible from obtaining better data* (to eliminate this vulnerability). Such an approach is a radical change from most current practices – both in identifying *which* data items are worth further attention (and which uncertainties simply do not matter) and *how much* it might be worth paying to improve the data quality in such cases.

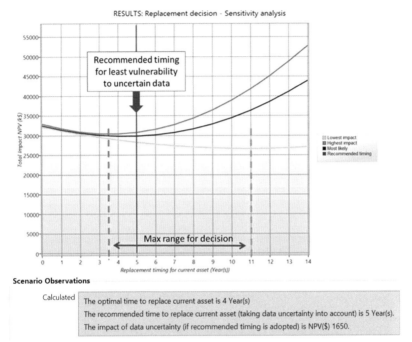

Figure 8. Evaluating the impact of data uncertainty

Note: In practice, it is very surprising how often the data uncertainty *does not matter*. From a significant range and diversity of practical case studies it is evident that, in about 80% of asset management decisions[4], a fully robust clear-cut decision and quantified business case can be made if the right questions are asked, of the right people, in the right way (capturing the range-estimates and uncertainties), and the correct maths (and sensitivity testing) is applied to determine the optimal strategy. In other words, in most cases we *already have the necessary information to make the right decision*; we just have to learn how to extract and use the knowledge correctly, and explore the uncertainties in order to focus on the ones that matter.

---

[4] Widespread field trials of SALVO processes in different industries, asset types and decision types.

3 Decision Support

"Trust me, I'm an expert" is not generally a reliable basis for determining what to do, when, and at what cost or risk. For many decades, however, technical experts have tried to make judgements about what designs would be suitable in the first place, how often to maintain them, what spares to hold, and when to replace them. And such asset experts have often had to fight for business credibility, defend against various stakeholder scepticisms and navigate a complex maze of financial, resource, regulatory or other constraints. This results in great inconsistency, subjectivity and short-termism. The silo'ed viewpoints and competing priorities, compounded by poor economic understanding, have meant that such decision-making has been expensive and ineffective in many cases. The human brain is good for many things, but it has proven to be particularly poor at choosing the right mix of risks to take, costs to incur and the best combination of short-term and long-term impacts. Almost any structured process or discipline can improve things. And the more critical or complex the decision, the more valuable and important is the use of a disciplined process, particularly one which is fact-based (objective) and correctly calculated to identify the best cost/benefit/risk option. At the highest levels of significant decision and complex strategy development, large investments in research, modelling and scenario evaluations can be worthwhile.

The opposite is also true, of course. For decisions that are both low impact and relatively simple, it is inappropriate to apply heavy disciplines and sophisticated analysis. There should be *proportionality* and recognition that decision-making methods (like any business process) should only be applied to the level of detail that is worthwhile.

When, for example, Reliability Centred Maintenance (RCM) was first spread from the airline sector to other industries, it was introduced as a process to determine what maintenance should be done *'for all failure modes of all equipment'*. Over 70% of such early implementations failed therefore, mostly due to the resulting 'analysis paralysis'. Subsequent maturity of understanding has recognised that criticality-selective use of RCM is essential, and that other (cruder but faster/simpler) methods have complementary roles for the low criticality parts of the asset portfolio.

RCM is an example of a *rule-based* method for decision-making, providing option choices for the appropriate type of maintenance activity, based upon seven questions and a multi-disciplined team consideration of equipment failure modes. Rule-based methods are the first step up from 'delegated common sense', as they introduce structured thinking, require multi-stakeholder inputs and create an audit trail for the resulting decisions. Such rule- or template-based methods have an important part to play but they are only part of the toolbox. They, and other levels of sophistication, are shown in Figure 9 and described below:

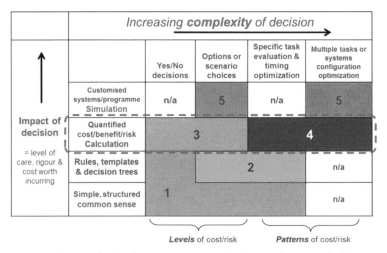

Figure 9. Decision support methods: toolbox needed

1. **Delegated common sense.** There are many decisions that should simply be delegated to informed and responsible personal judgement. Where decision consequences are low, and the choices simple enough, it is not necessary to introduce the delays, disciplines and costs of more formal methods. In such cases the costs of a 'heavier' process would outweighs the benefits of applying it (as the early adopters of RCM discovered).

However, even in this level of decision-making, great improvements can be made, primarily through education. In most organisations there is a big gap and inconsistency in the understanding of costs, risks, benefits and other business consequences. Teaching people simple value-for-money criteria, the financial impact of asset downtime and basic risk appraisal concepts can transform their decision-making abilities. Furthermore, the process of overtly delegating and trusting staff to make the right decisions (within clear boundaries of responsibility and decision authority) can yield big secondary benefits in motivation, pride and creativity.

And an audit trail is important even for the 'small and many' decisions; the training should be extended to ensure capture and documentation of three key elements that support a decision:
the **B**asis for the decision (assumptions and criteria used),
the **U**ncertainty in any of these assumptions and
the **S**ources of information that were used.

2. **Structured thinking and decision rules.** Slightly more important and complex cases clearly warrant a more objective, repeatable and independently auditable process. This is where decision-trees, rule-based methods, checklists and templates come in, sometimes using points scoring, weighted factors and other parameters to help in determining which way to jump, and how far. These are sometimes wrapped up into 'methodologies' and given brand names.

A number of such methodologies have emerged over the last 40 years, mostly from the highly structured, safety-critical or regulated industries - the armed forces, airlines and nuclear sectors. The developments of Integrated Logistics Support (ILS), Reliability Centred Maintenance (RCM) and Risk Based Inspection (RBI) are good examples. And further 'methodologies' and toolboxes, such as Total Quality Management (TQM, and its later manifestation, 6-Sigma), Total Productive Maintenance (TPM) and Lean methods have emerged from various manufacturing sectors.

In each case, a range of diagnostic and 'decision-support' disciplines has emerged to address endemic problems in operational reliability, risk, performance or cost efficiency. These have then spread as the application of such structured approaches were shown to be worthwhile. In many cases, there was an initial phase of over-enthusiasm and over-application, resulted in a number of expensive 'false starts' and disillusionments. Nevertheless, with better understanding of the limitations, selective application, and more attention to their implementation, they now form an important part of the asset manager's toolbox. Later in this chapter we will consider the strengths and weaknesses of some of these TLA ('Three Letter Acronym') techniques.

3&4. Calculation. For more complex decisions, and increasingly for *all decisions with any significant cost or risk implication*, the TLAs and points-scoring approaches are not enough. We have to talk in financial terms and make a 'business case' for what is worth spending, why and when. And, since many asset management decisions involve some form of trade-off between costs, risks and benefits, or between short term and long term effects, we need to find and demonstrate the optimal compromise. This means that value-for-money *calculations* need to be performed and the $$-sign introduced for quantifying the factors and their impacts. For example, RCM and RBI may help to select what *type* of maintenance or condition monitoring is appropriate, but they are poor, or even incapable of demonstrating *how much* to do (such as the optimal inspection or maintenance interval). This is frontier territory for many decision-makers, and requires a combination of training, structured decision processes and cost/benefit/risk calculations to find and to prove the best value solution. The necessary processes and tools will be discussed further in this chapter. They split into two significantly different types of approach:

a) **Cost/benefit/risk evaluation of 'step-change' options**, such as plant modifications or procedure changes, where the 'before' and 'after' can be characterised in terms of *levels* of cost, risk and performance.

b) **Evaluation/optimization of *cyclic* activities**, such as inspection, maintenance and renewal, where a *pattern* of cost/risk/performance needs to be controlled (and the evaluation involves a 'when' or 'how often' decision).

5. **Simulation**. The advent of fast computing has also introduced new possibilities for massive and complex modelling. Asset systems, asset behaviour, performance risks and economics can be simulated with increasing sophistication and precision, enabling, at a significant price of data collection and model development, very complex scenarios to be explored and evaluated (See Figure 10). Major investment options, with hundreds of thousands of component activities proposed across a large portfolio of assets, can now be modelled by high speed advanced simulation tools to seek the best basket of things to do, ranked against different business drivers or desired outcomes. It is easy to get carried away with such analytics, however, and lose sight of the human factors: ultimately it is people who make decisions, and there is a significant risk of poor understanding and acceptance if the recommended plan of action comes out of a 'black box' without being able to clearly demonstrate *why* the results are what they are.

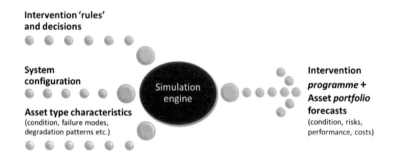

Figure 10. Typical portfolio modelling approach

3.1 The value of good data – a warning

Information systems enthusiasts regard almost any provision of data as 'decision support'. Certainly we aspire to 'fact-based' decisions, and data can help to sort out the facts from the subjective opinion, but we have to be very careful about this. It is easy to make things worse through data overload, creating more confusion than clarity, or by inappropriate use of data analytics or reporting tools that present attractive graphics but oversimplify or misinterpret the real situation.

As the methods to collect more and more data have grown easier and cheaper, many organisations are now swamped with data, yet are still complaining about not having the *information* they need to make the right decisions (see 'Addressing the data problem first' section 2.2.1). 'Big data' can hold big prizes, but it can also introduce big confusions, risks and costs.

In fact there are several different levels and contributions of data to decision support:

a) **Using data to *identify problems* and improvement opportunities**

The most obvious, and widespread role of asset data is to determine more objectively *"What and where are the problems?"* and *"How big are they?"* This is where historical evidence such as maintenance, performance and financial records can help to identify 'bad actors' and to prioritize our attention. Real-time information such as current asset performance and condition data, and Key Performance Indicators (KPIs) can also help to identify and focus on the genuine problems and improvement opportunities.

The choice of Key Performance Indicators (KPIs) to identify problems or improvement opportunities is a big subject and will vary greatly between assets and their environments. However the basic principle is simple: the objective is to detect existing or potential future problems and improvement opportunities in any of the dimensions of the Shamrock diagram. The significance of different dimensions varies, of course, with organisational context and the strength of different stakeholder interests. The collectability of hard evidence will also vary, with both practical factors (e.g. direct measurability) and value uncertainty (e.g. the significance of intangibles, and the volume of available evidence for low probability/high impact risks and for long-term sustainability).

Care is needed, of course, to avoid double-counting and yet to ensure adequate spread of coverage. Even in this role, where hard data is the obviously desirable basis for objective identification of improvement opportunities, the dangers of data overload are great: studies have shown that the human brain can cope with regular tracking of about 6-10 data elements; any more that this and the risks of confusion and missed warning signs increase rapidly.

b)   Using data to *explore the underlying causes* of problems
It is clear that hard evidence of unreliability, excessive cost or performance losses is useful in the *detection* and *quantification* of problems, but it is a very big step from locating the problem to the understanding of *why* it is a problem. Root Cause Analysis (RCA) seeks to drill down into the evidence in order to find the contributory factors that can be addressed, so that the problem can be reduced or eliminated in the future. However this requires understanding of relationships and cause/effect links.   Hard data alone is very unlikely to be able to demonstrate the relationships, whatever sophistication is applied in the data analytics. In fact one of the biggest 'data mining' studies done in the last 30 years[5] showed that there was only around 3% chance of being able to prove non-randomness (i.e. a correlation or a trend) from maintenance and reliability records alone.

c)   Using data as a basis for *forecasting the future*
Performance and condition observations and history data are extremely valuable as 'lagging' KPIs to discover problems that already exist. However the use of such data for extrapolation into the future and *anticipation* of problems is a much more difficult and vulnerable process. It requires understanding of degradation processes, the statistical significance of any trend or pattern that is perceived, and knowledge of external circumstances or factors that might be encountered. There are various analytical tools and methods to assist in this process but, like the use of data in RCA, great care is needed to combine the available hard evidence with common sense and asset expertise. Even with the recent advances in sophisticated asset performance and condition monitoring, the emerging hard data *alone* should not be the basis for forecast for future performance, risks or costs. Technical appraisal of asset health, for example, requires significant additional expertise to be converted into

---

[5] Shell Exploration & Production during the 1990s collated 10^8 maintenance work orders from their previous 20 years of operations in the North Sea, spent 2 years data cleaning and then analysed the results with a wide range of analytics and data mining tools. They found just 120 cases where the sample size of the same event was big enough to provide statistical significance and, among these, *only 4 cases where the pattern was provably non-random.*

forecasts of remaining asset life. Just relying on history and current condition data is like trying to drive your car along a highway *only looking at the rear view mirror and dashboard instruments.*

d) Using data to *evaluate improvement options*

This is the area where most data misinterpretation and misuse occurs. While hard evidence might be good for identifying, characterising or even extrapolating the *nature of the problem*, it is very rarely more than a partial contributor to the evaluation of *what to do* about the problem. Even with a clear, fact-based picture of the 'as is' situation, and data-supported forecasts of what would happen if we did nothing about it, we have to consider possible interventions and how much improvement they might achieve and potential risks they might introduce. So we are always facing uncertainties and partial knowledge; decision-support methods <u>must</u> incorporate techniques for handling speculation, 'what if?' considerations and fuzzy information about what might happen in the future.

3.2 A 'toolbox' approach to decision support

Supporting decisions about *what to do*, and *when*, is very different to the process of identifying and determining the nature of the problem. For such decisions we need to consider the degree of change that would be achieved by the intervention, the risks introduced, the secondary effects and trade-off's that will often be involved between dimensions of the Shamrock diagram. Furthermore, the correct procedures for such evaluations vary greatly with the type of intervention, or combination of interventions, being considered. So the processes and tools for decision-support must vary also – a *toolbox* approach is needed.

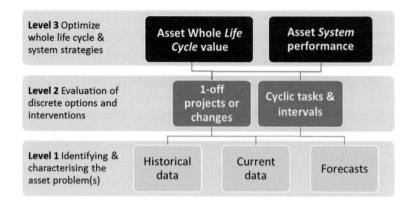

Figure 11. Compartments in the decision-support toolbox

Over and above the wide range of tools that exist to help identify and describe problems or improvement opportunities ('Level 1' in Figure 11), we are concentrating on the 'so what?' stages of decision-making that sit above them. In this role, there are four primary compartments to the toolbox (creating levels 2 & 3), corresponding to different complexities of the problem and techniques needed to make the right decision.

Level 2: addressed the evaluation of a **specific intervention**, such as a design modification, planned maintenance, condition assessment or asset replacement (*Is this task worthwhile, and if so when?*). This subdivides into two different methods required to address:

a) One-off tasks or 'step change' interventions, that comprise of a discrete activity that changes the level of costs, risks or performance (typically a 'before and after' study to evaluate cost/benefits and make a *Yes/No*, or *option A versus option B*, decision).

b) Cyclic tasks such as periodic inspections, maintenance or renewal, where the evaluation involves quantifying the pattern, and rate of change in costs, risks or performance (and a '*when?*' or '*how often?*' decision is involved).

Level 3: this is a higher level of complexity, in which tools and methods are needed to help evaluate the **optimal *combination* of solutions or activities.** Again, there are two variants in this:

a) Blending of the different activities performed on a specific asset over its life cycle (e.g. *Should more short-cycle maintenance be done to achieve longer asset life cycles*? or *How much should a mid-life refurbishment change the need for ongoing maintenance as well as extend the life of the asset?*):

b) Coordination and bundling of different activities performed for different reasons across different assets (e.g. *What is the optimal shutdown strategy for an asset system, given that different assets need different tasks with different urgencies?*)

These different decision types, and decision-support requirements, also align well with the needs identified in BSI PAS 55:2008, the Publicly Available Specification for Optimal Management of Physical Assets[6] (see Figure 12). And such methods also represent a rigorous demonstration of the required 'decision making criteria' for the ISO55001 standard for Asset Management.

---

[6] See www.PAS55.net

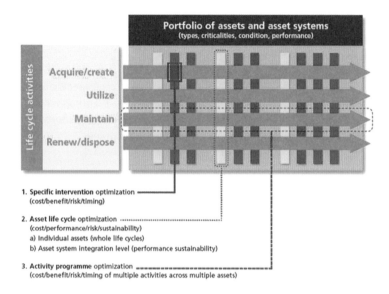

Figure 12. BSI PAS 55 requirements to optimize asset management strategies and plans

3.3   Structured approaches and methodologies

There are a number of 'methodologies' and valuable techniques for decision-support in asset management.   Each has its strengths and weaknesses, and most have evolved from specific industry environments and asset- or decision-type challenges.   Some have been more widely generalised and are now recognised to be standard elements in the toolbox.   For example, in the operations and maintenance decision-making areas, there are:

3.3.1   *Reliability Centred Maintenance (RCM)*

RCM emerged from the civil airline industry (MSG3 in the late 1970s).   It is a more prescriptive, rigorous extension of Failure Modes and Effects Analysis (FMEA), that gives us some logic 'rules' for determining what *type* of maintenance is appropriate, based on failure mechanisms and consequences.   It is particularly suited to complex plant where there are lots of failure modes: it provides a consistent navigation path with logical choice criteria for predictive, preventive, detective (failure-finding) and mitigation actions.

There is debate about various RCM flavours (e.g. the need to analyse all failure modes of all equipment, the role and methods of criticality-based targeting, the ways and viability of 'streamlining'), but the core value of RCM is undeniable: it is a concise summary of the questions that need to be asked in order to determine what type of maintenance is most technically appropriate.

Limitations:
Such methods (FMEA, RCM and also other 'risk-based maintenance' approaches) treat each failure mode individually and may miss some important combinational effects, such as the fact that a new risk may be *introduced* by a proposed maintenance activity. They are also *reliability-centred*, aimed at predicting, preventing, correcting or mitigating functional failures and their consequences. So RCM is not good at revealing tasks aimed to *slow down* degradation rates and extend life (e.g. painting or lubrication), or to raise/recover operational efficiency (e.g. cleaning of heat exchangers, de-coking of furnaces or changing of catalysts) where there is no discrete point of the asset having 'failed'.

RCM identifies the 'technically appropriate' maintenance method, but not whether the solution is the most *cost-effective* option, nor what is the *right amount* of the activities (e.g. interval or timing). Sometimes a cheaper but less technically correct strategy can provide better value. In others, a combination of methods may be justifiable to address a single failure mode. So it is neither safe nor correct to describe RCM as truly 'optimizing' maintenance. It can help greatly in selecting the right type of (maintenance) medicine for our assets but does not adequately help in determining the best dosage.

3.3.2   Risk Based Inspection (RBI)

Risk Based Inspection guides a systematic risk assessment of (primarily) high-criticality static equipment such as hydrocarbon-containment pipes and vessels, and the choice of appropriate condition monitoring methods. Developed as the American Petroleum Institute's Recommended Practice

(RP580/581), it is oil & gas industry-focussed. However cross-industry variants are appearing and scope has been extending to rotating equipment and other asset types. RBI's strengths lie in the systematic nature of the survey, the 'probability x consequence' view of criticality, the mass of technical data available about materials properties, degradation mechanisms and rates in different environments and the effectiveness of inspection or condition monitoring methods. It also introduces different levels of analysis, ranging from qualitative to 'semi-quantitative' and 'quantitative', depending upon the risks being considered.

So, where degradation mechanisms can be monitored, RBI is a proven and increasingly widely-applicable method for determining what type of condition monitoring is most suitable.

Limitations:
Despite the broadening range of asset types and degradation mechanisms covered, RBI is still most suited to high integrity assets in safety- or business-critical operating environments exhibiting a progressive and measurable degradation mechanism (e.g. corrosion). And even at the highest level of ('quantitative') analysis, the process is based on a scoring system derived from tables and 'factors'. So the results are better than direct subjective judgement, but do not quantify the economic risks or the effectiveness of proposed risk controls (inspection strategies) in business-quantified terms.

The inspection costs are often not considered within the RBI process, even if a system shutdown is needed to perform the inspection. This omission, and the embedded assumption that asset degradation will always to be at the worst possible rate, means that an RBI study will often recommend inspection intervals that do not represent the best cost/risk strategy. Like RCM therefore, it is not really correct to describe RBI as 'optimizing' inspection strategies: it can help in selecting the right health monitoring *method*, does not adequately help in determining *how much* monitoring to do, or *when to react* to the warning signs.

3.3.3 Total Productive Maintenance (TPM)

TPM encourages shared responsibility between maintainers and operators, attention to detail and a holistic 'Overall Equipment Effectiveness' (OEE) view. Emerging from the Japanese automotive industry, it has been used to achieve significant culture change, reliability and productivity improvements in the manufacturing sector. It introduces and encourages the concepts of 'autonomous maintenance' (operators perform simple asset health monitoring and first-line maintenance actions), cleanliness (which sets standards and a baseline for detecting problems), 'right first time' for work standards and 'one-point lessons' for continual improvement activities. TPM changes attitudes and delivers many 'quick wins'.

Limitations:
TPM does not introduce any specific tools or rules to determine which tasks are appropriate in the first place (where RCM is strong) and is fairly shallow in its consideration of reliability and asset-related risks (which is a vulnerability when introducing it to higher criticality/integrity assets and industry sectors). Nevertheless at least one oil company (BP) and some process industries have successfully adapted and implemented TPM processes with good results.

The OEE measure of 'success' is an element where such adaptation or extension is sometimes needed. As originally developed, OEE combines aspects of reliability, availability and quality, but it does not satisfactorily cover risks that have low probability and high consequence. Nor does it consider sustainability (e.g. equipment lifespan impact, or short-term versus long-term trade-offs).

3.3.4 Total Quality Management (TQM) & Six-Sigma (6-σ)

These are established, proven and thoroughly respected bundles of 'continual improvement' techniques. From Deming (via the Japanese manufacturing sector) and from Motorola respectively, TQM and 6-σ represent the push for quality and consistency in processes, in client-focus and in teamwork. They work through multi-disciplined 'quality circles', a statistical process control (SPC) toolkit and focussed improvement activities. They are also excellent catalysts for communication, clarifying objectives and fact-based decision-making.

If enough data is available, the TQM and 6-σ methods are good for revealing the 'quick win' and improved consistency opportunities and can help to establish a culture of continual improvement.

Limitations:
Many good intentions and initiatives are launched with these methodologies, but there is also a high drop-out rate and risk of 'temporary enthusiasm'. In part this is because TQM and 6-σ lack some of the essential 'teeth' – the specific solutions to handle the different situations and link the diagnosis of a problem right the way through to identifying and justifying of the best value action, and the right amount or timing of that action. The methods and tools are strongly oriented towards *high volume data* that can be analysed for patterns, trended and monitored with statistical significance. But most asset management problems and decisions are not supported by such data volumes.

In addition to their individual strengths and weaknesses, all of these methodologies suffer a further, final vulnerability. They are all poor at the final stage of value-for-money evaluation and the business case justification of what is worth doing, and when. In this area, however, two specific initiatives have addressed the questions that need to be asked and the steps required to be more consistent, quantified and transparent in asset management decision-making.

3.3.5   The MACRO Project

The first of these was a cross-industry European collaboration project in the 1990s. The MACRO (*MAintenance Cost/Risk Optimization*) Project[7] aimed to resolve the conflict between costs, risks and asset performance in typical intervention decision-making (see Figure 13). It was endorsed and supported by the European Union and UK Government as a 'best practices' initiative under the Eureka R&D programme (project EU1488). Participants included:

---

[7] European MACRO Project EU1488. www.MACROproject.org

Core Sponsors	**Partners**
Halliburton Brown & Root Ltd	Anglesey Aluminium Metals Ltd
National Grid Company plc	Asset Performance Tools Ltd
The Woodhouse Partnership Ltd	Det Norske Veritas
Yorkshire Electricity Group plc	ICI Eutech Ltd
UK Dept, of Trade & Industry	Institute of Asset Management
	National Power plc
	Norske Shell
	PDVSA Intevep
	Railtrack plc

In addition to the formal participants, a number of further organisations licensed the MACRO process and tools, contributing case studies and further industry feedback. These included Severn Trent Water plc, Northern Ireland Electricity plc, Score Valves Ltd, Sparrows Cranes Ltd, UK Paper plc, Conoco Ltd, BG Transco Ltd, Aylesford Newsprint and Aughinish Alumina.

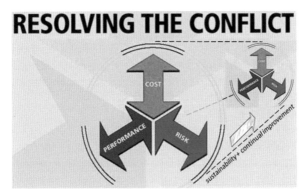

Figure 13. MACRO Project goal

The MACRO Project addressed a range of approximately 40 typical asset management decisions, developed some structured ways of considering the competing requirements, and produced various decision-support tools to assist in the quantification and optimization of the different intervention options. Most importantly, the research yielded a way of harnessing and quantifying expert knowledge (to supplement any hard data that may or may not be available) and of calculating the combined mix of costs, risks and asset performance for different decision options.

Much of the generic concepts and guidance (see section 2.3) on good practice decision-making in this guidebook comes from the original work of the MACRO Project.

Deliverables and impact of the MACRO Project

A suite of seven analytical software tools[8] was developed and field-proven, educational short courses were produced and piloted in many industries, dissemination events were held at all levels in most industrial sectors; over 30 technical papers and case studies were presented at national and international conferences, and the project completion seminar in London attracted over 70 companies, many at director level, to learn about the experiences and results that had been achieved. The project demonstrated the bottom line benefits of a structured approach, methods of quantifying the uncertain, intangible factors, and of calculating the optimal solution.

Sponsor observation:

"Effective decision-making is the key differentiator between organisations. We recognised in its early stages that the MACRO project had the potential to help deliver substantial advantage. Not only has this been realised, but we have enjoyed and benefited from the opportunity to share ideas with other 'best in class' organisations. The bottom line is that these tools are adding value to our business by enabling us to make rapid quantitative risk decisions in a robust, transparent manner. Tools like these are crucial enablers for our organisation, which aspires to achieve world class asset management."

Dr P. Jones, CEO, CE Electric UK Ltd. (formerly Yorkshire Electricity plc)

---

[8] Asset Performance Tools (APT). www.decisionsupporttools.com

Since then the MACRO processes and tools have been used in a number of organisations and industries around the world. The MACRO 'solutions', however, proved to have insufficient focus on process guidance and discipline. The tools and techniques were extremely effective in the hands of trained experts, but the natural triggers for initiating such studies were missing, and there was little guidance to establish the methods as normal, embedded decision-making processes.

In 2008, Asset Performance Tools Ltd, the developers of the APT software, was acquired by The Woodhouse Partnership Ltd with the objective of redeveloping and extending their capabilities into mainstream asset management, particularly addressing the surrounding *business processes*.

Furthermore, the subject of risk-based and life cycle cost optimized decision-making has grown to become a recognised critical business competency in the face of the global financial crisis, a widespread problem of aging infrastructure, asset knowledge losses through workforce retirements and age profiles, and increased expectations for corporate transparency, performance and rising standards of service. So a 'son-of-MACRO' collaboration project was launched in 2009 in order to research, develop and spread pragmatic guidance and best practice solutions – the SALVO Project.

3.3.6 The SALVO Project

The **Strategic Assets: Lifecycle Value Optimization (SALVO)**[9] project has been, like MACRO, a cross-industry, international collaboration to identify, document and develop good practices in the asset management decision-making – particularly in dealing with aging assets (degradation, obsolescence, renewal and optimal whole life cycle management).

Core sponsors:

- The Woodhouse Partnership (Project Managers)
- Scottish Water
- London Underground
- Sasol
- National Grid

Other participants in the project (providing technical support, field trials, peer review and validation) included:

- University of Cambridge
- Decision Support Tools
- Scottish Power Energy Networks
- Halcrow
- Sodexo
- Centrica
- Water Corporation of Australia
- AMT-Sybex
- ReflexTech
- Forbo Flooring
- IBM
- Institute for Manufacturing

---

[9] See www.SALVOproject.org

The SALVO Project ran from September 2009 to July 2013, with a number of work groups examining and developing best practices in different aspects of aging assets and their management. The resulting deliverables from the project comprise a combination of public domain guidance (including this guidebook) and case studies, detailed procedures and templates (a technical 'Playbook') and decision-support software tools (DST). The Playbook and DST software tools are now available under license, along with a full range of training courses and an international network of expert facilitators.

Observations from the participants:

The SALVO Project has helped us to identify and demonstrate the optimal timing of asset replacements and the optimal frequency for maintenance interventions. The outputs from SALVO are key components of our 'Asset Master Plans': we are now in the best place we have ever been.
Geoff Aitkenhead, Asset Management Director, Scottish Water.

SALVO is proving to be a useful tool in our armoury, providing a robust and consistent method of analysing complex asset investment decisions and providing a methodology of bringing diverse stakeholder groups together to jointly develop a solution.
Richard Moore, Head of Asset Management, London Underground

We were facing the apparently urgent replacement for obsolete equipment to the order of tens of millions of pounds. With SALVO we were able to reduce this by 60% and renegotiate support arrangements for the foreseeable future.
Christine Pretorius, Industrial Engineering, Sasol Synfuels, South Africa

SALVO allows us to communicate the basis of decisions to a range of stakeholders and, importantly, understand the impact of data quality on the decision.
Janet Ham, Capital Planning, Water Corporation of Australia

3.3.6.1 Project Scope

SALVO was targeted to provide practical guidance, procedures, checklists and decision-support tools for the optimal management of aging assets. This is not, however, limited to 'old' assets: aging (or degradation) processes can be rapid and can occur at any time, for a variety of reasons. Aging also includes the effects of obsolescence and technology overtake, rendering existing assets to be progressively less relevant, suitable or incurring higher ongoing cost or risks compared to alternatives.

The business requirements to make good decisions about such aging assets are fairly self-evident. The impact of error can be very great, and yet the likelihood of error is quite high (due, for example, to information uncertainty and the complexity of competing or interacting assumptions). Furthermore, it is difficult to be objective and consistent in the evaluation of very different options, such as a fair cost/benefit comparison between changing a maintenance strategy and a one-off 'project' to modify or refurbish the asset or to replace it. Life cycle costing, cost/benefit appraisal, risk analysis, financial discounting and reliability engineering calculations may be needed, and data availability will often be limited. This is why SALVO is so important – it helps us to navigate the issues, ask the right questions, evaluate the different possible actions and justify the correct interventions at the correct timings.

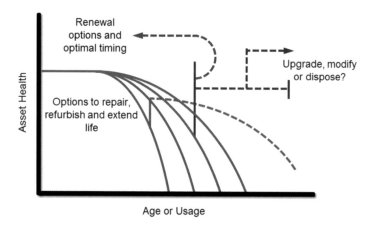

Figure 14. Decision challenges in management of aging assets

3.3.6.2 SALVO guidance

This guidance handbook is an important deliverable from the SALVO project. It addresses the practical issues being faced by asset-intensive organisations, with aging infrastructure, constrained resources and funding, competing priorities and rising stakeholder expectations. It summarises the decision-making guidance developed by the SALVO team, and provides case studies and illustrations of how these processes can be applied in different circumstances. Much more detail is also available, including a step-by-step 'playbook', with process maps, decision-support software tools, workbooks and templates, under normal commercial licensing terms or via expert facilitation and training from various project participants. See www.SALVOproject.org for more details.

3.3.6.3 Competencies framework

In the application of the SALVO processes, different levels of involvement, understanding and skills were recognised to be necessary. As the optimal decision must incorporate inputs from different parts of the organisation, it is vital that some level of understanding of the process, the outcomes and the optimization concepts is widespread: participants in the process need to understand what is needed and how their inputs contribute to the final decision – this greatly improves the 'sign-on' and acceptance of implications and commitment to the conclusions.

To lead a study, perform quantitative evaluations, explore the trade-offs, and 'what if?' scenarios, a study leader needs additional insight and competencies. Asset management decisions often involve quantifying probabilities and intangibles, estimating patterns of risk and navigating complex reliability, life cycle and economic modelling methods. And a study leader also has to have good interpersonal skills – harnessing the multi-disciplined inputs to achieve consensus and explainable outcomes.

There is also a 'super-user' level of understanding that is required to facilitate others in their decision-making. Expert facilitators are often valuable to support complex studies or programmes of study, or as occasional, call-in consultants. These individuals are not just good study leaders in a particular asset- or problem-type; they need to be able to facilitate the process *in any situation*, guiding others to solve their own problems and make their own decisions correctly. This further increases the need for interpersonal skills, deeper conceptual and modelling expertise, and mental agility to adapt generic principles to the different cases and circumstances. Commercial consultancy services, for example, require this level of competency to provide SALVO processes to their clients.

The competency framework is therefore supported by three levels of exam-tested certification:

a) **SALVO Process understanding**: SALVO Process awareness and concepts understanding – for intermittent involvement, informed contributions or affected parties (e.g. decision authoriser, endorser or implementer)

b) **SALVO Study leader**: SALVO Process detailed understanding, study team leadership, competent cost/risk evaluation/modelling of familiar decision types and asset types.

c) **SALVO Expert facilitator**: SALVO Process and facilitation expert, multi-skilled evaluator/modeller of a wide range of decision and asset types. Licensed SALVO consultants must be expert facilitators.

4 The SALVO Process

The overall SALVO Process is a top-down targeting of the key problems and needs for attention, followed by a bottom-up evaluation, justification and coordination of what is worth doing, when, to address these issues (see SALVO "Smiley" figure 15). In particular, it addresses some of the most critical cost-, performance- and risk-based decisions in asset management; decisions such as *"When should I replace this asset?"*, *"How much can I extend the life by a modification or refurbishment?"* or *"How much condition monitoring or maintenance is worthwhile?"*. These decisions frequently involve very uncertain assumptions about risk, performance impact and life cycle costs. Individual decisions also need to be considered in the context of competing priorities, budget or resource constraints and opportunities to bundle of work with other activities. It is also essential to develop a clear and credible business case in language that financial investors, safety managers, regulators and technical staff can all understand and accept.

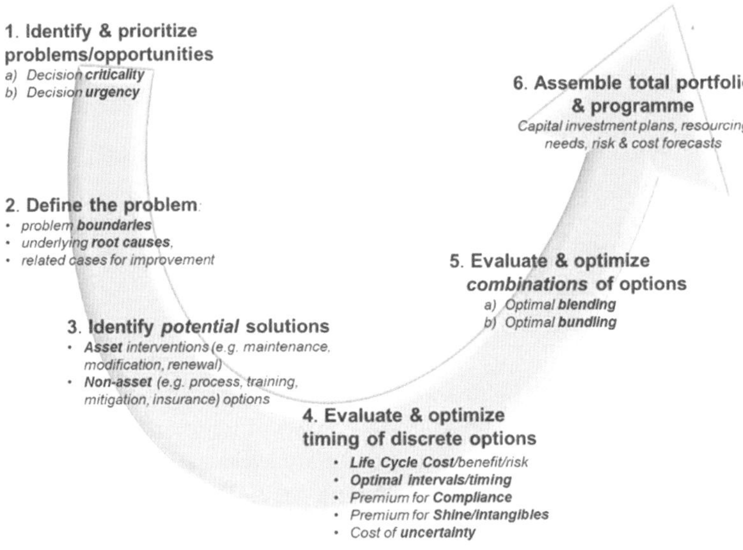

1. Identify & prioritize problems/opportunities
a) Decision *criticality*
b) Decision *urgency*

6. Assemble total portfolio & programme
Capital investment plans, resourcing needs, risk & cost forecasts

2. Define the problem
- problem *boundaries*,
- underlying *root causes*,
- related *cases for improvement*

5. Evaluate & optimize combinations of options
a) Optimal *blending*
b) Optimal *bundling*

3. Identify *potential* solutions
- **Asset** *interventions (e.g. maintenance, modification, renewal)*
- **Non-asset** *(e.g. process, training, mitigation, insurance) options*

4. Evaluate & optimize timing of discrete options
- Life Cycle Cost/*benefit/risk*
- Optimal *intervals/timing*
- Premium for *Compliance*
- Premium for *Shine/Intangibles*
- Cost of *uncertainty*

Figure 15. The SALVO "Smiley"
(illustrated version on inside back cover of this guidebook)

The SALVO approach breaks the subject up into 6 generic steps. They cover:

1. **Identify and prioritize problems/opportunities:** Identification of asset groups subject to aging characteristics and sharing similar criticalities and urgency of attention.
2. **Define the problem/opportunity:** Root Cause Analysis, drilling down to address the underlying issue rather than just treating the symptoms
3. **Identify *potential* solutions** that should be considered for each case or asset grouping – encouraging lateral thinking, including 'non-asset solutions'
4. **Evaluate and optimize timing of *discrete* options:** consistent cost/risk/benefit evaluation, including sensitivity analysis to uncertain assumptions and quantification of intangibles, impact of compliance etc.
5. **Evaluate and optimize *combinations* of interventions**
   a. Best *blending* of activities for the same asset/asset group (e.g. optimal mixture of inspections, planned maintenance, refurbishment and renewal timing for best life cycle value)
   b. Best *bundling* of activities for implementation and resourcing (e.g. shutdown strategy, work bundling opportunities etc.).
6. **Assemble portfolio and programme** and forecast cost, risk and performance implications.

4.1   SALVO high level process map

At the business process level, the SALVO Smiley can be flattened out in order to navigate the steps, the inputs required, and the various branches and routes that should be followed in different cases (figure 16). These processes are mapped and documented down to three further levels of detail by the SALVO consortium and these are available under license as a detailed Technical Playbook (along with the SALVO decision-support software tools) from a network of accredited suppliers and service providers[10].

---

[10] See www.decisionsupporttools.com

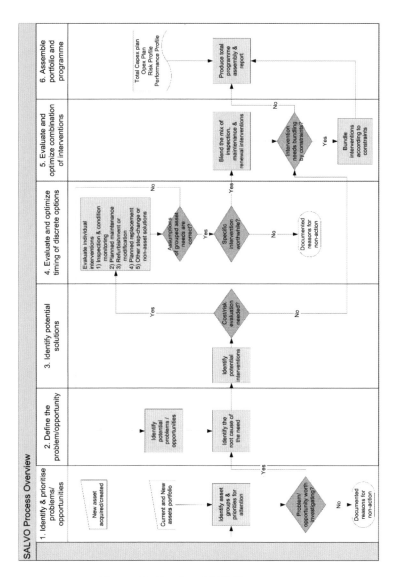

Figure 16. Top level SALVO process map

4.2   Different SALVO starting points

This overall SALVO process is very flexible – there are several possible starting points, depending upon the decision requirements (see figure 17). The Smiley handles the systematic and prioritized development of management strategies for a diverse population of assets (starting at Step 1) or the analysis of an *individual* asset management problem/improvement opportunity by joining the process at Step 2. Or, if you want to jump straight to the evaluation of proposed interventions (e.g. a discrete project evaluation, or cost/risk/benefit ranking of a range of proposed projects, or a systematic review of current maintenance activities, or prioritization of an asset renewals programme), you can start at Step 4.

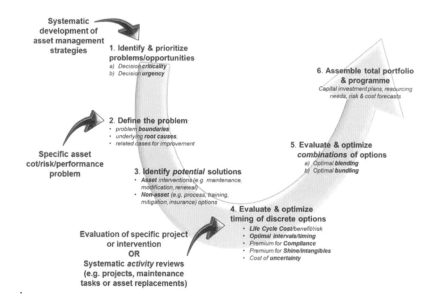

Figure 17. Different uses and starting points for SALVO process

Common starting points for the SALVO processes are therefore:

A) Systematic development of asset management strategies (e.g. review of existing assets and their condition, deterioration and maintenance, life extension or replacement needs).

This is the 'first principles' approach, targeting the most important, widespread and urgent cases for attention in an asset portfolio. In particular, it uses Step 1 to identify groups of assets for shared characteristics and common need. This provides the necessary targeting logic and prioritization of attention. Step 2 then defines the issues more systematically, diagnoses the underlying risks, vulnerabilities, costs and performance concerns, so we solve the problem rather than just treat the symptoms. Thereafter, Step 3 identifies possible treatments, which are evaluated individually in Step 4 and collectively in Step 5, before being assembled, with the other activities justified for other parts of the asset portfolio, in Step 6. So the full SALVO 'Smiley' has been used to guide a top-down targeting of the improvement opportunities and what is worth doing, and when, followed by a bottom-up assembly and optimization of the resulting asset management plans.

B) Specific asset problems or improvement opportunities
If an asset-related problem, 'bad actor' or improvement opportunity is identified (for example, a failure has occurred, or asset condition/performance has deteriorated, or an obsolescence notice received from a vendor, or a new technology upgrade has come onto the market) then a discrete decision is needed about what needs to be done about it. SALVO Step 2 is the logical starting point in such cases, forcing consideration of the nature of the problem/opportunity, its boundaries and root causes, including identification of other cases that might be similarly affected (and benefit from similar review). Thereafter, Step 3 encourages consideration of a broad range of potential preventive, corrective, mitigating and risk management options to address the issue. Each potentially viable option can then be evaluated to identify the best value solution and optimal timing, either as a discrete solution (Step 4), or as a combination of actions (Step 5) before being merged appropriately into the many other activities requiring resource, budgets and work management (Step 6).

C) Evaluation of a specific intervention OR systematic reviews of asset management activities
Sometimes it is desirable to jump straight to the evaluation of specific actions or a range of proposed activities (such as a review of maintenance tasks, a range of project proposals, or programme of asset replacements). In these cases the starting point is either Step 4 (if the tasks are pre-

identified and merely need to be evaluated/prioritized), or Step 3 if they need to be challenged and alternatives considered. In both cases, this bypasses the consideration of root cause reasons for attention; it presumes knowledge of the underlying problems and prior selection of the actions or interventions that are worth considering. This method jumps directly to the evaluation of 'is this activity worth doing and, if so, when?.

This requirement can be encountered both in individual cases (such as "Shall I refurbish this specific asset, or replace it?"), and in batch programmes of study, such as the review and optimization of maintenance, spares or asset replacement strategies. SALVO provides processes, tools and guidance for the discrete cases that can be handled simply and clearly, and also for larger programmes of 'batch' review to be prioritized and managed efficiently, using criticality prioritization, templating and 'batch' evaluation facilities.

5   Step-by-step guidance

5.1   Step 1: Identify and prioritize problems/opportunities

The first SALVO step involves two main processes:

a)   **Segmenting** the population into discrete asset groups for which a shared asset management strategy is appropriate.

Segmentation is required to split down a portfolio of assets, or asset systems, into groups of assets that are likely to have similar asset management needs.   Such groupings will share not just physical attributes (e.g. asset types) but also functional criticalities, condition, performance and other attributes that might affect costs, risks, performance and the need for asset management interventions.   This chapter provides guidance on the possible grouping criteria and the use of such criteria in determining how to segment an asset population into suitable groups for the purpose of developing optimized (life cycle) asset management strategies.

b)   **Prioritizing** the resulting groups, to ensure that the highest impact, most urgent cases are addressed first and with greatest rigour.

The asset groups, once identified, will have widely differing needs and opportunities for operation, inspection, maintenance, spares, modification, refurbishment, decommissioning and renewal.   They will also have different priorities for attention and potential impact of good or bad asset management.   So the second part of SALVO Step 1 involves the determination of both the **importance** of doing the right things (i.e. *criticality* of decisions and interventions) and the **urgency** of doing the right things (i.e. *timing*, and *sensitivity in timing*, of decisions and interventions).

5.1.1 Segmenting an asset population

There is wide variation in understanding about the setting of asset management strategies for different asset types. It is still common to find organisations applying standardized strategies for different asset classes, relying on vendor recommendations, inflexible 'engineering standards' or generic asset-type studies. More mature businesses recognise the importance of customising such strategies to take account of the asset's functional roles, business criticality and operating context (e.g. operational flexibility and redundancy). But, as in most areas of asset management, there is a trade-off involved; personalising the strategy for each individual asset should achieve greater value over the asset's life cycle, but the effort to do this will often be greater than the benefits obtainable. So the practical approach is to develop strategic plans that will have a broad applicability (i.e. one strategy can be applied to many instances), but not so generic and standardised that they will cause inappropriate activities, or intervention timings, to be performed in some cases.

To get the balance right, we need to segment the portfolio of assets into groups that share enough characteristics and circumstances to be reasonably considered as identical, and for which it is therefore suitable to develop and apply a common asset management strategy. The resulting group sizes may range from one (a unique asset in unique circumstances, warranting personal attention) to thousands (where a template or generic strategy is consistently applicable).

So how do we perform the segmentation? What features can we use to distinguish assets and their differences in likely management requirements?

There is a long list of *potential* factors that could affect the groupings, but typically only four or five factors will be needed to characterise a unique set of circumstances and asset management requirements. The obvious ones include:

a) **Asset type, configuration and model** – these determine many of the performance capabilities, vulnerabilities, potential degradation mechanisms and risks.

b) **Functional role and criticality** – the operational/business consequences of failure or performance losses, and therefore the degree of care worthwhile to ensure reliability.

c) **Asset condition, performance and 'health'** – the existing state or, even more importantly, the rates of change and actual degradation patterns.

Additional factors to be considered include:

d) Manufacturer/supplier interchangeability (supply chain dependency and therefore risk)

e) Asset size/capacity, especially in relation to forecast demand

f) Usage/operational loading e.g. throughput volumes, types of product or service, variability in loading, operating cycles

g) Installed system-level capacity/standby/redundancy and operational flexibility (affecting functional criticality)

h) Complexity and interdependence with other assets within interconnected systems (e.g. networked assets versus discrete individual units).

i) Location and environmental exposure e.g. indoor/outdoor under/over ground, coastal/polluted vs arid/clean location

j) Age: calendar time and/or operating usage e.g. due to atmospheric corrosion or physical wear mechanisms affecting age

k) Technology change rates e.g. obsolescence risks and timescales

l) Applicability of legislation, non-negotiable policies and standards, and any likely changes in these

m) Fixed installation or mobility/interchangeability

n) Capital value e.g. high intrinsic or resale value assets may warrant greater value protection

o) Ease of physical assess (e.g. for maintenance), geographical location/distribution

p) Online maintainable, or only offline (shutdown-based) access.

q) Asset owner/operator/maintainer and contractual service provider context e.g. who has what responsibility for asset investment, asset performance and asset care.

> **EXAMPLE:** defining an asset group
>
> A population of 4,500 electrical protection relays comprises a mix of mechanical, electro-mechanical and electronic designs, of varying ages of installation, providing a protective function to a variety of different electrical equipment distributed across a network of different asset systems.
>
> SALVO Step 1 Segmentation would split the population of relays into:
>
> a) the three easily distinguished **technology types** (mechanical, electro-mechanical and electronic).
> b) within two of these relay types (mechanical and electro-mechanical, which tend to be the older installations, and more vulnerable to age-related and mechanical deterioration mechanisms), further segmentation into a series of **age bands** or (if data available) reliability/performance bands.
> c) within the resulting types and age/reliability matrix, a further segmentation is necessary to distinguish the different **criticalities** of their installed locations (e.g. level of damage to the electrical systems if the protective relays do not operate when needed).
>
> The total population of relays is now provisionally segmented (this will be challenged and refined later in the SALVO process) into specific asset groups such as:
>
> *"Mechanical units, 20-30 years old,*
> *in category A criticality roles"*

5.1.1.1 'Digital' differences and 'analog' ranges

The segmentation of a large portfolio of assets, with an unknown diversity of needs, can be intimidating. So the best way of arriving at practical groupings is to perform the segmentation in two stages. Firstly, using *whatever clear-cut hard data can be obtained*, sort and filter the lists by 'digital' differences – the factors that can be easily classified as category A/B/C, Yes or No, configuration x, y or z. Examples of such digital differences include the type or make of asset, whether it has installed backups/redundancy, is situated indoors or outdoors etc. This stage of segmentation can usually be performed by a non-expert, under simple instruction for the relevant data filters and manipulation. In Example 1, the digital differences were based on asset type (protection relays), then sub-type (mechanical, electro-mechanical, electronic).

Next come the factors that require expert judgement – the 'analog' scales of potential difference in asset management needs. These need to be turned into discrete ranges or bands of likely difference. So deeper knowledge of asset characteristics and their operational contexts is required. For example, what levels of performance, or age bands, or operational criticalities should be treated as sufficiently different to justify personal asset management attention (i.e. different asset group membership)?

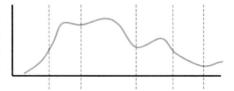

In Example 1, the analog differences were the age bands and the functional criticality bands, both of which needed to be selected for their likely differences in asset management implications. Someone had to decide that 20-30 year old relays constituted a cohort of similar-state assets and should be treated differently to, say, 10-20 year old units. Similarly, 'Class A' criticality had to be defined as a recognizable feature of certain assets that warrant a similar level of attention.

Normally only three or four such characteristics will be both easily available data and have a distinguishing influence on the urgency of intervention. And the combination of these features identifies specific asset groups that can be expected to share risks, vulnerabilities, performance characteristics and asset management strategies. And such asset groups can include anything from just a single, unique circumstance asset to a very large number of 'similar' units for which a shared strategy represents a big multiplier of cost, risks, performance and sustainability effects.

Note: At this early stage in the SALVO Process, the grouping of assets into likely 'shared asset management needs' is only provisional. The groups identified in this way are not final – they are working assumptions in the development of likely 'common template' strategies. In the subsequent SALVO steps, such as the identification and evaluation of intervention options, we will find that some groups need to be split down further, while others can be combined into larger groups if it transpires that one of the factors used for splitting assets into different groups does not, in fact, make any difference to their optimal asset management strategy.

5.1.2 Prioritizing assets or asset groups for attention

Even with a good segmentation, a portfolio of assets will often yield a significant number of asset groups requiring case-by-case consideration and different management strategies. With limited resources and competing demands in most organisations, it is essential therefore to sort out which asset groups are the highest priority for investigation and attention.

Many organisations already realise that assets in different functional roles have different criticalities and that this has a profound influence in how they should be managed. However 'criticality', or importance to the organisation, is just one dimension to be considered. Assets can be critical but stable, or they can be less critical *now*, but subject to increasing risk, or technology overtake/obsolescence, so there is an *increasing* criticality or concern. A second dimension is needed therefore; the timing-sensitivity or urgency of attention (see figure 18). The highest priority for our attention must therefore be a combination of <u>criticality</u> (importance of making the right decision) and <u>urgency</u> of attention (consequences of delay in making a decision).

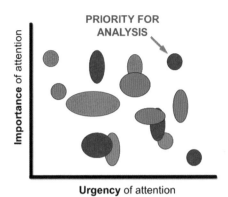

Figure 18. Prioritizing assets or asset groups for analysis

5.1.3   Scaling the 'importance of attention'

The need for optimized asset management strategies is certainly closely related to asset **criticality** or **value** to the organisation. This corresponds, directly or indirectly, to the business impact of the decisions being made (the potential consequences of getting it wrong).   Such scaling of significance takes two primary forms:

- Static or **capital value** – if the asset is intrinsically valuable (in the balance sheet or buy/sell sense), then the importance of asset care, and resisting any loss of value, is clearly high. A valuable asset is worth protecting and justifies careful decision-making.

- Dynamic or **functional value** – the *usage* of an asset represents the value to the organisation.   So asset condition and performance need to be protected/maintained and the right decisions made about what to do, and when. Note that this is commonly described as **asset criticality**, and is often represented by the business consequences of functional failure or unplanned downtime.   Nevertheless it may not be limited to *failure* consequences: it might be a level of operating efficiency, 'lost opportunity' or performance constraint *relative to new technology alternatives* (i.e. obsolescence). The wider definition of criticality, for the purposes of ranking the importance of making the right asset management decisions, should take account of all stakeholder impacts, and both internal and external vulnerabilities. These are discussed below.

5.1.3.1 Asset Criticality

Much is written about asset-related risk and asset criticality, with significant confusion remaining. However, if we strip the concept down to the basics, what makes an asset important (critical) is that it has, or has the potential for, great business impact. This aligns with the ISO55000 definition of an asset:

"**Asset:** Item, thing or entity that has value or potential value to an organisation"

And 'value to the organisation' can manifest in many different forms, reflecting the interests of different stakeholders (Figure 19). The neatest summary of this, and clarification of *methods available to quantify the value*, was developed by the European MACRO Project introduced in chapter 3.3.5. The Shamrock diagram (see section 2.3.1) has an outer ring of typical stakeholder interests, and an inner five dimensions representing the different ways of scaling their significance.

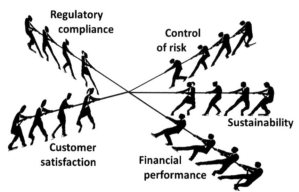

Figure 19. Competing views of 'criticality'

The Shamrock five methods of quantifying impact can be used in combination to define asset (or asset group) criticality:

- **Risk:** specific events, such as equipment failures or safety incidents, scaled by probabilities x consequences. This is the most common feature used in defining asset criticality, however many organisations only consider the potential consequences of failure, irrespective of probability. This is acceptable for prioritizing *reactive* work (e.g. urgency of reinstating normal function) but not really adequate for scaling the importance of developing *proactive* strategies, where a reduction in failure probability and/or mitigation of failure consequence needs to be considered.

- Operational **Efficiency:** the ratio between inputs (e.g. operating costs), and outputs (e.g. asset performance). So *inefficiency,* such as restricted performance, service level or high operating costs, is also a potential contributor to asset criticality.

- Operational **Sustainability:** asset life expectancy and the benefits of avoiding or deferring capital expenditure. This is very difficult to incorporate into an asset criticality ranking because it represents future potential impacts.   It can, however, be converted into the present day value of future cashflows through an amortized capital value, derived from an expected economic/realisable life.

- **Compliance**: this can be scaled indirectly as the 'premium paid for compliance' by assessing the costs of what *must* be done for compliance reasons, compared to what would be otherwise justified for risk, operational efficiency or sustainability reasons.

- **Intangibles** or **'Shine'** factors represent reputation, customer impression, employee morale etc. (involving human perception). These are scaled, like compliance motives, by indirect, inference methods; the 'premium paid for Shine' is the difference between what we would *like to do* (for Shine reasons), and what a more objective consideration would otherwise have justified.

5.1.3.2 Scales of impact

When quantifying criticality, either as a simple scoring system or more explicitly in terms of economic significance, there are a number of practical considerations that increase the credibility of the results.

- Points, scores or quantified economic significance are all much better than 'linguistic variables' (words, such as High, Medium, Low) to differentiate between asset or asset group criticalities. Numerical methods are much better, however because we can align, combine and rank numbers more easily, and this improves consistency in assigning significance and enables us to assemble a 'total criticality' from different aspects of importance.

- Ranges, rather than absolute values, in each of the Shamrock dimensions can help to compensate for data unavailability or uncertainty provided that the ranges are sufficient to distinguish between asset circumstances. Ranges or bands can then be converted to points or scores that represent median values to maintain proportionality.

- Ranges, and the points or scores that are used to represent them, should be non-linear (i.e. not 1, 2, 3, 4). Scales of impact are often very non-linear and, to ensure correct ranking of dissimilar assets, a proportionate scoring or points contribution is needed (points being ascribed on a consistent basis such as $1000 of impact = 1 point).   In the case of risks, this requirement goes further still, especially for the low probability/high impact events, which need to be *disproportionately* represented to account for the inherent uncertainties in this zone[11].

5.1.3.3 More than just a risk matrix

The development of a corporate risk register and risk matrix (see Figure 20) is a good starting point for the risk element of criticality, but usually

---

[11] This requirement for disproportionality is incorporated into the UK Control Of Major Accidents and Hazards (COMAH) legislation.

needs to be extended to cover other aspects of the Shamrock diagram (risk is not the only 'importance' consideration).

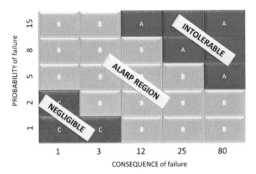

Figure 20. Typical 5x5 risk matrix, showing the cost/risk 'trade-off' zone (ALARP = As Low As Reasonably Practicable).

Another vulnerability of a risk matrix for 'importance ranking' is the common simplification used in creating a single scale of event consequences. Such a matrix is excellent for rapid risk ranking but, for the sake of simplicity, each event is typically scored on the worst single outcome of financial, safety, environmental or performance consequences, rather than a potential *combination* of these. So it can be difficult to represent a risk that has a moderate financial AND safety AND performance consequence.

An example of criticality definition, incorporating risk elements and other dimensions of asset importance is shown in Figure 21. **Note:** each organisation will have a different mix of dominant business drivers, so the different parts of the Shamrock diagram will have different manifestations and scales of significance.

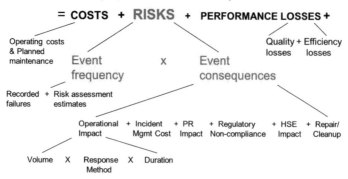

Figure 21. Example of criticality formula for asset systems, asset groups or individual assets.

The individual contributors to such a criticality calculation need proportionate and recognisable ranges of impact and scales of significance. Non-linearity must be considered, and the 'fuzzy' value of some factors (e.g. reputation impact, safety or customer satisfaction) should be calibrated with a scoring system that equates to a standardized value of, for example, £1,000 = 1 point (see Figure 22). Factors which are difficult to quantify, such as 'Shine', can be scaled indirectly – by estimating what the organisation would be willing to pay *not* to have such impact.

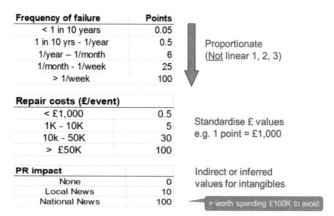

Figure 22. Example of scales of impact (each organisation must calibrate their own)

This approach to criticality scoring is highly 'scalable' – it can be applied to systems, sites, assets, components or individual risks or problems, with appropriate adjustments to the ranges and points used. Whatever level of application, however, the resulting criticalities show a very consistent Pareto distribution (see Figure 23). Typically 5-10% of the items/issues are extremely significant: indeed these are usually already known – you could have identified them simply by asking around. Then a larger volume (typically 30-50%) of the items/issues are sorted and ranked by net importance: this is where the rigour of approach is so vital – providing more objective ranking of many items, each apparently core to the business. Finally there is a long 'tail' of high volume, but individually low criticality items/issues.

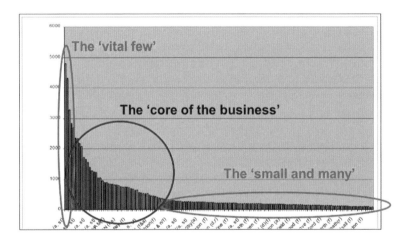

Figure 23. Typical criticality analysis results (assets, issues, sites, processes)

5.1.3.4 Asset group size

The final consideration in scaling criticality and the value of developing an optimized management strategy is that of asset group size. While an individual asset may have a particular importance and justify our attention, a population of identical assets in very similar functional roles can share a single analysis and strategy development effort – this is the concept and reason for asset grouping in SALVO Step 1. And, if a single strategy can be developed for, say, 50 near-identical units in similar circumstances, we get 50 times the benefits of the analysis effort and decision-making. So we need to consider asset group size in the ranking of which asset groups to consider with what priority. In simple terms, the group size can be used as a multiplier for any score or points ascribed to individual asset within the group (all members of the group must, by definition, have the same or very similar individual criticality).

5.1.4 Scaling the 'urgency' of attention

The second dimension in prioritizing which assets or asset groups to study, is the timing sensitivity or urgency of attention. Assets may be very critical but stable, or they may be less significant currently but expected to deteriorate rapidly, or be rendered obsolete or redundant in the future. The prediction of when asset replacement is likely to be needed for example, or some other intervention will become necessary, is an approximation for this 'attention urgency'. Some options for scaling this axis are:

- **Age or Utilisation measures** – either a direct measure of asset age (difference between 'design life' and actual age), or an inferred 'residual life' estimate from more direct measures of condition or utilisation. Only if degradation is understood to be directly age-related, and no better information is available, should simple calendar time can be used. If degradation mechanisms are more closely correlated to asset utilisation, then operating hours or counts of operating cycles, throughput or other measures.

  Better still, if the data can be collected and collated, are the composite measures of 'effective age'. For example, 'Effective Operating Hours' are used for an industrial gas turbine to schedule major overhauls or module replacements. These are calculated formulae based on a combination of normal operating hours, the number of stops and starts (which stress the turbine through thermal cycling) and the 'peak load hours' that also accelerate the aging process.

- **Asset Health** – a customised combination of age, condition and performance characteristics used to approximate to the aging or degradation processes, and thereby adaptive to the likely remaining useful life. Note that, in cases of monitoring asset condition or performance over time, the *rate of change* is more important than the current state for the purposes of extrapolating forwards to indicate residual life.

An asset health score or index may be made up of any combination of the following information – the key criterion being that the net figure should be as close as possible to a direct measure of likely urgency of major intervention (e.g. asset replacement).

Condition Testing or Measurements	Failure frequency	Operating costs
Condition Monitoring	Service experience	Energy costs
Operating Performance	Condition discovery	Facilities support costs
Defect History	As-found condition	Customer complaints
Fault history	Asset repair costs	Quality & Volume
Performance compliance	Extraordinary maintenance needs	OEE
Reliability	Maintenance history	Normalised fault rate
Post mortem forensics	Planned maintenance frequency & history	'Black swan' vulnerability (to low probability, high consequence events)

Table 1   Possible asset health measures

- **External events on the horizon** – useful asset life can be curtailed by changing circumstances, and it is important to consider any such factors looming on different timescales. For example, technology overtake or vendor liquidation can render current assets 'obsolete' (increasing risks and repair costs as spares become more difficult to obtain), or some vital natural resource may be expiring (e.g. mineral or petrochemical reserves).

External factors that can represent a threat to ongoing useful/economic asset life include:

- Changing stakeholder expectations (e.g. customer, investor, regulator)
- Forecast changes to asset functional demand
- Technology overtake/obsolescence
- New legal/other absolute requirements
- Cost of money (interest rates/taxation impact/exchange rates)
- Budget limit versus rising costs
- Energy prices
- Labour: resourcing, competencies, demographics, employment constraints
- Climate change
- Finite resources/feedstock availability
- Competition
- End of operating license
- Raw materials or supply chain vulnerabilities

5.1.5 Combining importance & urgency

The available evidence will vary widely, but the SALVO discipline requires us to identify and use the combination of 'importance' criteria and 'urgency' criteria to determine which issues should be prioritized for attention. Figure 24 shows typical examples of such information, including how the same information can sometimes be used in more than one way (e.g. asset health data helps to rank the criticality dimension and also, if we can obtain 'rate of change' evidence, the urgency dimension).

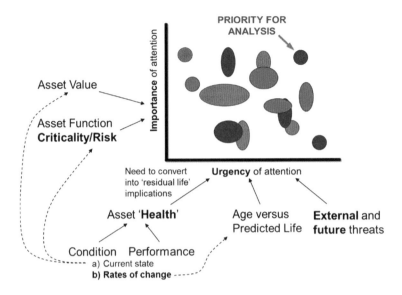

Figure 24. Combining criticality, asset health or other data to scale importance & urgency

Once the asset groups have been identified and prioritized, it is time to explore the nature of the problems they face, and the options available to alleviate, prevent, recover or mitigate the consequences of these problems. Steps 2 and 3 of SALVO will explore the nature of the problems faced (or opportunities that exist), and identify potential actions or interventions that should be considered.

5.2   Step 2: Define the problem

Having identified which asset(s) to address with what urgency in Step 1, we start to explore the prioritized cases. In Step 2 we will clarify the *nature* of the problems being faced – not content with the apparent symptoms, we need to consider the underlying issues and seek opportunities to eliminate the *cause(s)* of the problem rather than just controlling the effects.

Step 2 is also the starting point for *one-off cases* that do not require the proactive identification and prioritizing of multiple issues in Step 1. The self-evident discrete cases might represent specific 'bad actor' assets causing urgent concern. Or perhaps it is a group of assets that clearly requires attention, either through their own degradation, risks or performance problems, or due to some external decision 'trigger' such as a vendor notice of discontinued support (obsolescence), or an operational problem/risk encountered by other users. An important integration requirement for SALVO is the identifying and connecting of such decision triggers to the initiation of the right steps of the SALVO process, *as a normal part of business operations.*

Step 2 comprises the following required activities:

a)   Problem definition statement
b)   Root cause analysis
c)   Identification of other cases sharing the same root cause vulnerability

5.2.1   Problem statement

Whatever the starting point (via SALVO Step 1 targeting of assets and issues to address, or direct to this Step 2 point with a self-evident problem to solve), we need a clear definition of the case to be considered.   This provides focus and alignment for the participants, and makes sure we develop solutions or improvements that are relevant and effective. Also, for this purpose, it does not matter whether the case is a 'problem to solve', or an 'improvement opportunity' to investigate – in either case, we need to be clear about its *nature* and its *boundaries* before we consider what might be worth doing about it. This is best expressed in a clear Problem Statement.

A problem statement is a short descriptive combination of text and, wherever possible, illustrations, which defines the problem to be solved or improvement opportunity to be explored. The statement should:

- Be based on facts (not opinions or assumptions)
- Be short (ranging from a short paragraph to 1 page maximum)
- Describe the characteristics of the current problem or situation
- Identify the systems and process context (e.g. role of assets affected)
- Describe the scope of the problem (assets, systems, business processes)
- Describe the ideal outcome or desired condition
- Quantify/estimate the business impact of what is at stake (impact of not addressing/potential benefits of improving)
- Identify affected stakeholders and their interests/expectations
- Specify what it is *not* – within reason.

5.2.2   Root Cause Analysis

Once the issue is more clearly identified for scope and context, we consider the underlying reasons for its existence. This is known as Root Cause Analysis (RCA) and is a familiar process in many organisations for post-mortem analysis of asset failures or other incidents. However, in SALVO Step 2, we also use the methods in a *proactive* way: even if no specific incident has yet occurred, we can apply the same thinking to identify the potential underlying causes of an anticipated problem, such as degradation-related major failures, or non-compliance with future legislation, or spare parts unobtainability due to supply chain problems.

There are many RCA techniques available. The SALVO project did not therefore feel it necessary to develop new techniques in this established field. However, the proactive use of the tools represents a significant change in established thinking and requires us to use them in a different manner.

RCA is a primarily a fact-based technique and much effort is sometimes needed to obtain and consider evidence of the problem context, observed symptoms and cause-effect relationships. Several of the methods encourage a multi-disciplined brain-storming to create hypotheses, which are then challenged and tested against the available evidence. This 'hypothesis' approach is also particularly valuable in proactive RCA, when structured speculation and expert judgement are often required to compensate for the lack of available hard data.

In other cases, there might be plenty of raw data and the challenge lies in extracting useful information from it. The data might have inconsistencies or unknown quality, or be held in different forms and locations, so patterns and correlations are difficult to spot. If the data volumes and quality are good enough, then 'data mining' techniques can be useful to seek and quantify trends, correlations and statistical significance. For example, many Computerised Maintenance Management Systems (CMMS) or Enterprise Asset Management (EAM) systems, contain vast quantities of planned and unplanned maintenance records, asset condition and performance data, costs etc. Similarly, operational control systems, condition monitoring systems and inspection records can be invaluable. But do not forget also to incorporate direct operational knowledge from operators and maintenance staff. In many cases this can provide short-cuts to the real underlying problems, or identify/qualify/correct data errors. We still need to challenge any subjective judgement inputs, but asking the right questions of the right people can often provide rapid focus on which factors to investigate.

Note: The world of 'data analytics' is developing very fast, with the greater ease of collecting Big Data. However, while this is good news in the detection of problems and improvement opportunities, there are some fundamental weaknesses in what these methods can achieve in root cause analysis. For example, no matter how much data is collected about asset failures, the history often reflects only a partial view of the underlying risk patterns. For example, if there is any condition-based or planned maintenance being performed, we are 'censoring' the experiences of what would happen if the asset were *not* maintained – yet this is the very information we need to justify such (preventive) interventions.   Historical data analysis, on its own, therefore often reveals apparent randomness in the events, in which case asset expertise and local operational knowledge are required to consider possible relationships, correlations and failure mechanisms.

The SALVO consortium concluded that, at very minimum, the RCA methods that should be considered are the 5Y's and the 5M's.   This corresponds to asking 'Why?' at least five times to drill down into the causes, and using the 5M's as a checklist of types of cause to consider at each level.

5.2.2.1   Five levels of digging

The 5Y's is a technique whereby the analysis team ask the question 'Why?' repeatedly until an underlying, treatable cause of the issue is found.   An example of this is shown in Table 2.

Observed problem	Bag filter blocked
Why? #1	Pre strainer corroded/failed
Why? #2	Pipe leak (gasket failed)
Why? #3	Flange bolts not tightened properly at last re-fitting
Why? #4	Tensioning check not performed
Why? #5	**Work order not specific enough**

Table 2.   Example of 5Y's

The table shows that, for the failure mode 'Bag filter blocked', the lack of clear instruction to tension flange-bolts was the 'root' cause.   Of course, it is possible to go further down into the reason for this omission and indeed academic studies[12] have shown that it can take many iterations of asking 'Why?' before reaching a genuinely indivisible systemic root cause. However this would lead to analysis paralysis and not add any real value

---

[12] Managing the Risk of Organizational Accidents, J.Reason 1997

to the process. The first 3-5 levels of digging into 'Why' usually reveal some tangible opportunities to intercept the chain of events and prevent the 'top level' event.

5.2.2.2 Five directions in which to dig

The 5M's is technique used to classify the potential *types* of cause. It helps us, at each level of 'Why?' to think laterally and consider the combination of factors that might be involved in the causation chain. The 5M's stem from work done in the Japanese quality management processes, and is often represented in a fishbone, or Ishikawa diagram. The 5M's consider different potential areas of cause contribution:

- **(hu)Man**
  - o   Was the cause a manpower/human factors issue?
  - o   Were they competent, motivated, informed?
- **Machine**
  - o   Was the cause a machine-related problem (equipment/hardware/component defect)?
  - o   Did it involve 'normal' wear and tear, incorrect calibration, a hostile usage environment (outside operating envelope) or incorrect maintenance?
- **Materials**
  - o   Was the cause a raw materials, feedstock or utilities supply issue?
  - o   Was the quality of the material/input acceptable?
  - o   Were the spare parts correct?
- **Measurement**
  - o   Was the cause a measurement, reporting or diagnosis issue?
  - o   Was the frequency and type of measurement correct, and is the accuracy of measurement acceptable?
- **Method (process or method of operation)**
  - o   Was the cause a method or process suitability or stability issue?
  - o   Were the start-up, operations and maintenance instructions correct?

There are a number of possible reasons for the intermediate cause identified in Table 1 at the 3rd Why? *"Flange bolts not tightened properly"*. Examples of proposed next-level causes for this are shown for each of the 5 M's in Table 3.

'M'	Possible cause for *"Flange bolts not tightened properly"*
Man	Technician was not trained to do the task properly and did not follow the work order to include a tensioning check.
Machine	The pneumatic tool which was used to tighten the bolts was not working properly.
Materials	The bolts were of the wrong specification which caused them to elongate under stress.
Measurement	The calibration of the tension wrench might be wrong – or wrongly read.
Method	The tensioning check might have been omitted in the work instruction.

Table 3. Examples of 5M's considered at the 3rd level of Why?

The 5Y and 5M techniques are combined in the SALVO recommendation, with a feedback loop as evidence is sought to validate or reject each potential cause (see Figure 25).

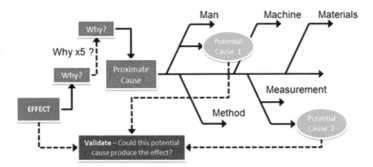

Figure 25. Combining 5Y's with 5M's (Ishikawa Diagram)

The objectives here are to

a) Avoid just dealing with the symptoms, by identifying, attacking and ideally eliminating the underlying causes.

b) Stimulate lateral thinking about a wider range of potential cause contributors, so we do not automatically just blame people or the equipment.

If this process is performed sensibly, without reaching the 'analysis paralysis' level of micro investigation, we usually find several intermediate or root causes that can be addressed through proactive elimination, reduction or mitigation (controlling their effect) actions.

5.2.3   FMECA - organising the information

The assembly of the various issues to be addressed is often done in a tabular format. Failure Modes, Effects & Criticality Analysis (FMECA) is a method of characterising the individual problems in terms of why and how they occur, their local and wider (system) consequences and their significance (likelihood x consequence = level of risk).   There is quite a skill in clearly and concisely describing individual failure modes, problem causes and their different effects and consequences. As a practical tip, the most useful descriptions will identify both the *component* that fails and the *mechanism* by which it fails – e.g. a functional failure of a pump might be caused by failure modes such as "bearing seizes due to lack of grease" or "impeller jams due to foreign object ingress". Figure 26 shows an example of a FMECA worksheet.

Facility	MegaProc Site A
System	Cooling System
Asset / System	Cooling Water Pump
Manufacturer	Jacksons Ltd
Model / Type	CCW 120ltr
Year of Manufacture	2006

Prepared by:

Approved by:

Function/s	Functional Failures (how can the asset lose its function?)	Failure Modes (what causes the functional failure?)	Failure Effects (what happens when the failure mode occurs?)	Criticality — Effect Category	Criticality — Risk assess if NOT Hidden or S&E — Risk Score	PROPOSED TASK for Prevention/Risk Control	Frequency (Hours, Days, Weeks, Months or Years)	Trade (Operator, Technician)	Asset Running Stopped	Estimated Time required in minutes
1. To transfer water from Tank A to Tank B at 80 - 100litres/minute	A. Unable to transfer any water at all	1. Bearing seizes due to lack of grease	Motor trips out and trip alarm is sounded on the building control panel. Tank A low level alarm sounds after 30 minutes, and tank runs empty after 45 minutes. Downtime required to replace the bearings is 4 hours.	EO	16	Lubricate the pump bearings with one pump of Grease 4456	6M	T	R	10
		2. Impeller comes off due to loose nut	Motor does not trip but pump stops. Tank A low level alarm sounds after 30 minutes, and tank runs empty after 45 minutes. Downtime required to replace the shaft and impeller is 8 hours.	EO	20	Inspect shaft and replace if female impeller thread is damaged. Replace the impeller holding nut with a Self-Locking type and torque to the correct setting.	Not applicable	T	S	480
		3. Impeller jammed by foreign object that had got through a damaged filter.	Motor trips out and trip alarm is sounded on the building control panel. Tank A low level alarm sounds after 30 minutes, and tank runs empty after 45 minutes. Downtime required to clear the foreign object is 2 hours.	EO	8	Remove, clean and inspect suction line filters. Replace if there are any signs of damage.	1M	T	S	30
		4. Coupling shears due to excessive fatigue, due to misalignment	Motor does not trip but pump stops. Tank A low level alarm sounds after 30 minutes, and tank runs empty after 45 minutes. Downtime required to replace the coupling is 4 hours.	EO	10	Carry out Vibration analysis to detect for mis-alignment. Arrange for the coupling to be re-aligned if required.	3M	T	R	30
	B. Transfers less than 80 litres/minute	1. Impeller worn due to age	Tank A Low level alarm sounds. Downtime to replace impeller is 4 hours.	EO	4	Install low & high flow alarm to detect low water flow. And check its calibration every 12 months.	12M	T	S	120
		2. Partially blocked suction line filters	Tank A Low level alarm sounds. Downtime to unblock the suction line filters is 30 mins.	EO	8	Remove, clean and inspect suction line filters. Replace if there are any signs of damage.	1M	T	S	30
2. Must contain the water and keep its temperature	A. Pump leaks water	1. Mechanical seal failed due to fatigue	Water leaks on to the floor and then down floor drain. Downtime to replace mechanical seal is 4 hours.	ESE	Not applicable	Visually check pump for water leaks. Report any leaks found.	1W	O	R	10
	B. Insulation is missing	1. Insulation has been physically damaged and fallen off.	Very hot pump casing is now exposed. Energy usage will increase. Downtime to replace insulation is 1 hour	ESE	Not applicable	Visually check pump for secure insulation. Report any damage found.	1W	O	R	11

Failure Effect Categories

Evident Functional Failure	Hidden Functional Failure
Evident Safety & Environmental (ESE)	Hidden Safety & Environmental (HSE)
Evident Operational/Customer Service effects (EO)	Hidden Other (HO)
Evident Non-operational effects (EN)	

Figure 26. Example of FMECA worksheet

© TWPL 2012

Some organisations combine this stage with the selection of what to do about each problem i.e. use the same table to record the proposed preventive or risk control task. In practical terms this is a sensible use of the multi-disciplined team expertise that is typically assembled for such studies. But the content can be improved considerably if the SALVO Step 3 Menu is considered for this – and potential *alternative* options and possible *combinations* of options are also identified. If a single 'solution' is chosen straight away, there is a significant risk of jumping to a (technical) conclusion without enough lateral thinking. However, provided that the Step 3 Menu of options is actively considered, then a single consolidated summary of the problems (and the various potential solutions) is a useful part of the documented audit trail to underpin asset management strategies.

5.2.4 Identifying other cases vulnerable to same underlying problems

Before Step 2 is complete, however, now is the time also to consider *which other assets are vulnerable to these same underlying causes or failure mechanisms.* If the same issue is encountered elsewhere, then fixing the problem might have wider benefits. And, as SALVO is trying to improve the business justification for what to do, then any scope for secondary benefits should be considered in the evaluation of options.

There are two ways of handling this:

i) Just record the secondary opportunities for now, and stick with optimizing the strategy for the currently selected asset group. Any other assets that benefit from the resulting strategy will be considered in their turn – albeit now with some useful pre-work done in identifying some of their vulnerabilities (their Step 2 stage will be easier).

ii) Reconsider the asset groupings to include the other cases that are now identified to be similarly affected by the selected root cause.

However this method should *only be considered if the resulting broader asset group could be managed by a shared strategy* i.e. the other differences in asset condition, health, circumstances etc. are small relative to the identified (common) root cause of the concern that you are trying to address.

Identifying such other assets is not always easy. This takes a form of 'RCA in reverse': in this case we are starting with a selected cause (or anticipated cause, in the case of proactive RCA), and then considering which other assets or functional circumstances would be affected by such a vulnerability or weakness.

5.3   Step 3: Identification of possible actions or options

Once a specific asset or group of assets (in similar condition, criticality and other circumstances) is selected, and its/their shared problem or improvement opportunity clearly identified, the next step is to consider the different interventions, risk management or improvement options which might be possible. SALVO Step 3 involves considering a wide 'menu' of such potential solutions, stimulating lateral thinking and making sure that we do not leap to conclusions about what should be done.   In some cases, this step actually identifies solutions that do not involve any expenditure at all, or triggers ideas about changes in our operating regime, communications, training programmes or other 'non-asset' interventions.

The goals of this step are to select all reasonable solutions that are worth exploring and evaluating, and to reject the impossible or self-evidently uneconomic/impractical options.   So this is an initial filtering process, without yet doing any quantified cost/benefit evaluation, or considering the degree of effectiveness, or timing of the interventions.   Its value lies in the forced consideration of approaches or options that might not otherwise be thought of. And it considers a much wider spectrum of options than the activity-specific 'strategy development' and 'decision support' methodologies (RCM, for example, guides the selection of one of only five 'maintenance strategies' in addressing a risk or failure mode). The SALVO 'menu' includes over 40 different possibilities to consider (see table 3).

5.3.1   Solution selection: principles

Two principles are important in this option selection stage:

- Many possible actions **do not involve direct asset interventions**. In fact nearly half of the potential options on the menu are not directed at the assets themselves – they address operator competency, stakeholder expectations, contingency plans etc. Engineering or technical staff often have a bias towards engineering or technical solutions (e.g. maintenance, modification, refurbishment, renewal, decommissioning etc..).

SALVO Step 3 helps to stimulate a wider consideration of how to eliminate, control the risks or reduce the effects of the problem.

- In a disciplined consideration of different ways (or combinations of ways) to make an improvement, the **lowest cost, least intrusive options should be identified and considered first**. When faced with 'aging' asset problems, it is easy to presume that asset renewal or at least a major refurbishment or intervention is needed, but it is remarkable how often a simple solution can be found to extend asset life, reduce risk and defer major expenditures. Although Step 3 does not include the *evaluation* of the options, it is important to identify any possible simple solutions at this stage, as well as the big investment options.

The guidance offered by existing methodologies such as RCM and RBI tends to take a simple branching 'decision tree' approach. Based on a series of questions (seven of them in the case of RCM), a mutually exclusive choice of strategies is presented. In the case of RCM, seven such questions lead to one of five 'maintenance strategies' such as failure finding tasks (for hidden failure modes), predictive maintenance (condition monitoring), preventive maintenance, run-to-failure (corrective maintenance) and 'proactive' interventions such as an equipment design modification. This approach has the benefit of simplicity, but is not good at stimulating lateral thinking, identifying *non-technical* solutions or the possible *combination* of solutions that may be appropriate. The SALVO 'Menu' approach (see Table 4) is not so simple to apply (we have to consider a longer list of possible options) but it does trigger insights and innovative solutions that do not always require (maintenance or capital investment) expenditure.

5.3.2 The menu of options to consider

		Possible Y/N	Action/option to be considered
1 Acquire/Create	1.1 Select/acquire/create new asset (to meet new demand)		
	1.2 Select/acquire/create new asset (replace existing) & timing		
	1.3 Change technical specification for acquiring/creating		
	1.4 Change supplier/constructor		
2 Utilize	2.1 Change operational parameters		
	2.2 Change operation (duty, loading)		
	2.3 Change operational procedures		
	2.4 Improve operator competence		
	2.5 Improve operator motivation/recognition'		
	2.6 Change buffer stock/capacity		
	2.7 Change outsourcing/insourcing of asset operation		
	2.8 Outsource asset function		
3 Maintain	3.1 1-off asset health assessment		
	3.2 Periodic non-intrusive inspections & interval		
	3.3 Periodic intrusive inspections & interval		
	3.4 Continuous condition/performance monitoring		
	3.5 Periodic functional testing & interval		
	3.6 1-off maintenance/refurbishment & timing		
	3.7 Periodic preventive maintenance & interval		
	3.8 Planned corrective maintenance & condition threshold		
	3.9 Run To Failure corrective maintenance		
	3.10 Change spares holding		
	3.11 Improve maintainer competence		
	3.12 Improve maintainer motivation/recognition		
	3.13 Change maintenance procedures		
	3.14 Change outsource/insource of maintenance		
4 Change/improve	4.1 Modify asset (change level of cost/risk/perf)		
	4.2 Refurbish asset (change degradation rate & extend life)		
	4.3 Change asset configuration		
	4.4 Change asset functional location/usage		
	4.5 Change outsourcing/insourcing of changes/improvements		
5 Renew/dispose	5.1 Replace existing asset (like-for-like) & timing		
	5.2 Replace existing asset (incl upgrade/downgrade) & timing		
	5.3 Change outsourcing/insourcing of asset renewals		
	5.4 Decommission and mothball		
	5.5 Decommission and salvage spares		
	5.6 Decommission and dispose		
6 Contingency plan	6.1 Manage stakeholder expectations (e.g. risk appetite)		
	6.2 Aquire asset technical data		
	6.3 Create Emergency/Business Continuity plans		
	6.4 Take out insurance		
	6.5 Adjust asset valuation/criticality		
	6.6 Diversify supply chain		

Table 4. Step 3 menu of possible actions to consider

5.4 Step 4: Evaluation of Individual Interventions

Having identified the asset(s) we are most concerned about (Step 1), clarified the issue(s) we are addressing (Step 2), and selected the possible improvements we might be able to make (Step 3), we have now reached the heart of the SALVO process: the disciplined evaluation of the costs, risks and benefits of these options, and development of a clear-cut business case for doing the right thing(s), at the right time.

This is the step where historical practices, habits and subjective judgement often distort our perspectives. There is also plenty of data uncertainty to cope with, as well as competing priorities and the conflicting expectations of different stakeholders. And we must consider various practical constraints (e.g. financial, human and physical resources, geography and access) to ensure that our proposed solutions are, in fact, deliverable. SALVO Step 4 addresses all these challenges, and introduces some simple, navigable processes to reduce the subjective bias, eliminate many of the commonest errors and greatly improve both the transparency and the consistency in justifying what is worth doing, why and when.

Step 4 is therefore important and the SALVO Project had to develop a number of innovative methods, both at the human factors level (psychology, discipline, team-collaboration techniques) and at the technical level (trade-off calculations, optimization, sensitivity analysis etc.). In particular it established a rigorous **process** basis for such decision-making, in the form of a set of 'storyboards' for the different decision types.

For example, the storyboard that is appropriate to evaluate an **asset modification** (minor design change) requires us to characterise and quantify the proposed project, the current asset attributes, the changes in costs, risk, performance that we anticipate, any costs or risks *introduced* by the change, any timing or execution constraints (such as a limited horizon of possible benefits), plus financing considerations, uncertainties etc. This is a very different sequence and set of questions to those needed for, say, evaluating the optimal testing interval for a safety protection system, or the level of critical spares to hold. Such decision-specific storyboards ensure that:

a) The **right questions** get asked (for the option being evaluated).

b) Of the **right people** (invariably the information needs to come from different disciplines and sources of expertise).

c) In the **right way** (see section 2.3.2 Collecting and using expert knowledge).

d) And the **appropriate calculations** are performed – instantly, so that 'what if?' ideas and data uncertainties are immediately evident in terms of decision impact (this is vital for decision credibility).

In relation to the level of decision-making rigour (see 'proportional sophistication' Figure 9), SALVO Step 4 has concentrated on the 'quantification, calculation and business case justification' methods, since these are generally poor and/or inconsistent in most organisations. Note, however, that these methods are also entirely complementary to simpler, rule-based methods (e.g. RCM, RBI – see Figure 27): the SALVO techniques can be used to quantify and challenge/refine and justify the outputs of such studies.

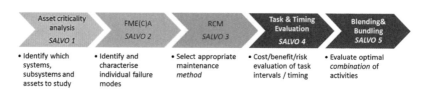

Figure 27. SALVO process applied to maintenance optimization

Similarly, in cases where greater, customised modelling and scenario simulation is justifiable (at typically, an order of magnitude extra cost and effort), the SALVO Step 4 processes can 'feed' such models, providing much greater rigour, credibility and 'drill-down' auditability of the underlying task justifications and timing sensitivities.

Starting at Step 4

Step 4 is also the starting point for either a single-case direct evaluation of a proposed intervention, or a systematic study of pre-identified/proposed activities (such as an investment programme, or revision of planned asset replacements) or current activities (such as planned maintenance and inspections). This short-cut to the 'evaluation' stage presumes that such tasks exist for good reasons, which we will now try to quantify, challenge, evaluate and prioritize. This process will confirm and clarify the business case for activities that are worthwhile, provide a value-for-money basis for prioritization, and will demonstrate which, if any, are *not* worthwhile.

Furthermore, the SALVO process, using the tacit knowledge capture methods described in section 2.3.2, combined with instant 'What if?' evaluations, often identifies improvement ideas that would not otherwise have been considered. However it is important to recognise that such an approach cannot rigorously identify new activities that might be worthwhile, or offer better value/effectiveness than the ones being considered. The only safe way to consider new needs or alternative interventions, is to start at SALVO Step 2 (problem definition), leading to Step 3 (potential solution identification).

Different solutions need different evaluation methods

SALVO has grouped the options and potential interventions into families according to the type of evaluation that is needed – the questions that need to be asked, and the mathematics involved in the cost/benefit, risk, life cycle and financial calculations. At the highest level, this splits out the options into:

a) **One-off changes** that make a permanent difference or that change the *level* of cost, risk, performance etc. Examples of this type of evaluation include design modification projects, changes to operating strategy, competency programmes and risk mitigation options (insurance, spares held etc.). In almost all these cases, a common approach to 'before' and 'after' modelling is possible, creating scenarios to explore different options and variants.

However the SALVO consortium did find it worthwhile expanding this capability for critical spares decisions; to seek the optimal numbers to hold and evaluating different vendor options, storage locations, pre-installed standby versus warehouse inventories and other spares-related decisions.

b) The **cyclic activities** that address *patterns* of cost, risk, performance etc. and involve a 'when?' (or 'how often?') decision. For these cyclic activities, the evaluation methods then further subdivide into the individual storyboards needed to optimize:
   a. predictive inspections and condition monitoring,
   b. failure finding tasks (e.g. functional testing),
   c. planned or preventive maintenance
   d. asset replacement: optimal life cycles with either 'like-for-like' renewal or design change/upgrade.

Table 5 below shows the appropriate evaluation methods for each of the different options that might have been selected in Step 3. Note that the simplest level of one-off Change Evaluation is the most commonly suitable method. Note also that in some cases, this evaluation might also be used as a rapid pre-screening technique even for apparently cyclic activities (usually just long-cycle tasks such as asset procurement/replacement): if the decision proves marginal or has high impact, it can then be escalated to the full asset life cycle modelling and exploration of decision consequences.

			Evaluation method
Acquire/ Create	1.1	Acquire/create new asset (replace existing)	Lifespan renewal LCC
	1.2	Acquire/create new asset (in addition to existing)	Project/Change > LCC Eval
	1.3	Change technical specification for new assets	Project/Change Evaluator
	1.4	Change supplier/constructor	Project/Change Evaluator
Utilize	2.1	Change operational parameters	Project/Change Evaluator
	2.2	Change operation (duty, loading)	Project/Change Evaluator
	2.3	Change operational procedures	Project/Change Evaluator
	2.4	Improve operator competence	Project/Change Evaluator
	2.5	Improve operator motivation/recognition'	Project/Change Evaluator
	2.6	Increase buffer stock/capacity	Inventory Optimizer
	2.7	Change outsourcing/insourcing of asset operation	Project/Change Evaluator
	2.8	Outsource asset function	Project/Change Evaluator

Maintain	3.1	1-off asset health assessment	Project/Change Evaluator
	3.2	Periodic non-intrusive inspections	Inspection Evaluator
	3.3	Periodic intrusive inspections	Inspection Evaluator
	3.4	Continuous condition/performance monitoring	Inspection Evaluator
	3.5	Periodic functional testing	Inspection Evaluator
	3.6	1-off maintenance/refurbishment	Lifespan LCC + refurb.
	3.7	Periodic preventive maintenance	Maintenance Evaluator
	3.8	Planned corrective maintenance	Maintenance Evaluator
	3.9	Run To Failure corrective maintenance	Maintenance Evaluator
	3.10	Change spares holding	Inventory Optimizer
	3.11	Improve maintainer competence	Project/Change Evaluator
	3.12	Improve maintainer motivation/recognition	Project/Change Evaluator
	3.13	Change maintenance procedures	Project/Change Evaluator
	3.14	Change outsource/insource of maintenance	Project/Change Evaluator
Change/ improve	4.1	Modify asset (change level of cost/risk/perf.)	Project/Change Evaluator
	4.2	Refurbish (change degradation rate & extend life)	Lifespan LCC + refurb.
	4.3	Change asset configuration	Project/Change Evaluator
	4.4	Change asset functional location/usage	Project/Change Evaluator
	4.5	Change outsourcing/insourcing of changes/improvements	Project/Change Evaluator
Renew/ dispose	5.1	Replace existing asset (like-for-like)	Lifespan renewal LCC
	5.2	Replace existing asset (incl. upgrade/downgrade)	Lifespan renewal LCC
	5.3	Change outsourcing/insourcing of asset renewals	Project/Change Evaluator
	5.4	Decommission and mothball	Project/Change Evaluator
	5.5	Decommission and salvage spares	Lifespan renewal LCC
	5.6	Decommission and dispose	Lifespan renewal LCC
Contin- gency planning	6.1	Manage stakeholder expectations	Project/Change Evaluator
	6.2	Acquire asset technical data	Project/Change Evaluator
	6.3	Create Emergency/Business Continuity plans	Project/Change Evaluator
	6.4	Take out insurance	Project/Change Evaluator
	6.5	Adjust asset valuation/criticality	Project/Change Evaluator
	6.6	Diversify supply chain	Project/Change Evaluator

Table 5. Evaluation methods for different intervention options

5.4.1 Decision support tools for evaluation and timing optimization

SALVO also commissioned the development of a suite of decision support tools (DST) to guide us through the decision-type 'storyboards' and perform the relevant calculations and timing optimizations for these different options. This modular toolkit covers Steps 4, 5 and 6 of the SALVO Smiley. The Step 4 modules and their primary usages are shown in Figure 28.

Decision support tools

DST PROJECT/CHANGE EVALUATOR

One-off projects or changes to assets ('step-change' modifications) OR changes in procedures, competencies, standards, resourcing, risk mitigation or risk transfer.

DST INVENTORY OPTIMIZER

Spares, materials, supply chain and purchasing options, operational standby-by & redundancy options,

DST INSPECTION EVALUATOR

Condition assessment, inspections, predictive maintenance and functional testing activities & intervals

DST MAINTENANCE EVALUATOR

Planned preventive maintenance, planned maintenance intervals, corrective maintenance, performance/efficiency improvements, life extension activities

DST LIFESPAN EVALUATOR

Asset replacements, optimal renewal timing, major refurbishments to extend life, new asset design options (life cycle cost evaluation)

Figure 28. Decision Support Tools: Step 4 Evaluators

The following sections discuss and illustrate the evaluations that are necessary to produce a robust business case for different options.

5.4.2   One-off Projects and Change Evaluations

The most basic of evaluations is the process and calculation needed to determine a simple Yes/No decision about a single discrete action. If there is a <u>level</u> of costs, risks, performance or other 'Shamrock' elements, and a proposed action will cause a change in this level, then cost/benefit appraisal will involve a 'before and after' calculation of the amount of change that can be achieved in return for the costs involved. Yet even at this simple level there are common errors and inconsistencies, such as those often encountered in the handling of 'small projects'; for example, it does not take long for staff to realise that including 'safety' in the justification increases the chances of the project being approved.   So the priority here is to establish a transparent, universally applicable discipline and screening procedure that can be used to evaluate individual cases, and can also enable ranking and filtering of a range of cases (to demonstrate the best value options).

5.4.2.1   The process

The cost/benefit evaluation process brings together the costs of the proposed change, the 'before' and 'after' levels of cost, risk or performance, and any constraints that may exist (see Figure 29).   The calculation of value-for-money must take into account any data uncertainty, and include sensitivity analysis to identify factors that most affect the decision: this helps us rapidly to identify what data is worth collecting, to what levels of accuracy, in order to reach a robust conclusion.

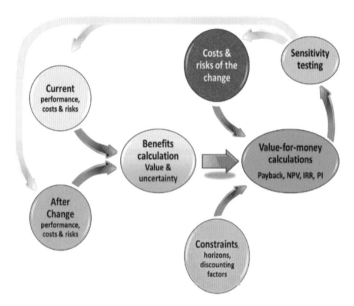

Figure 29. Evaluation process for one-off projects and changes

The SALVO storyboard (see Figure 30) walks us through this process. And, to save a great deal of data entry, the 'after-change' situation can be created simply by duplicating the current one and then editing and annotating only the data that is expected to change. Once the project itself, the 'before' and 'after' situations, and any overriding constraints are described, the value-for-money can be determined, along with the effects of data uncertainty, and the 'premium paid' for any compliance or Shine factors (intangible etc).

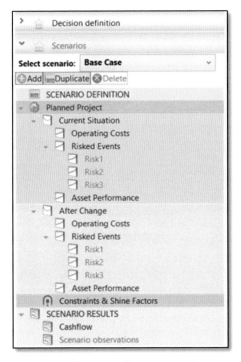

Figure 30. Storyboard for a simple project or change evaluation.

The main challenge in these cases is to establish greater consistency and business discipline in the face of wide variations in project types, data quality, time available and capital expenditure constraints. Estimating costs, risks and benefits can be difficult, particularly if 'intangibles' are involved, or the impact of a proposed change is based on uncertain forecasts and assumptions. Similarly, the capture and quantification of expert knowledge needs careful psychology – not just in *what questions to ask* (to ensure that each idea/project is considered against all the Shamrock dimensions), but also in *how to ask them*, so that the information is captured with minimal bias or distortion (see section 2.3.2 Collecting and using expert knowledge). In many cases it is better to start with a range-estimate and explore whether or not greater accuracy is needed (see Figure 31).

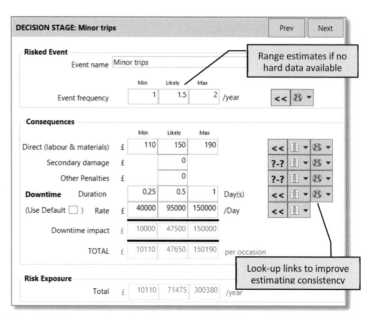

Figure 31. Range-estimating data entry with look-up and estimating aids

The basis and origins of the data, or range-estimated expert knowledge, also needs to be recorded. The audit trail is a vital part of decision credibility, so notes on the Basis, Uncertainty and Sources of information (BUS) must be captured *at the time of the quantification*. It is much harder to retrofit these explanations after the study. DST tools provide, for each 'frame' of information, a dynamic notepad in which to record the BUS details.

Note: Minor trips > Description

Basis
Ops are reporting 1-2 problems/year. This aligns with the maintenance history in last 2 years.

Uncertainty:
1-2 events/year but highly variable duration; typically 8 hrs but could be 4-24 hours (worst case)

Information Source:
Bill Reedback (Ops Supervisor, 12 yrs) plus production records from Maximo CMMS

Once the structured assembly of best available knowledge has occurred, the decision-making process involves calculation of typical value-for-money indicators, such as Payback Period, Net Present Value and other decision-making criteria. These enable projects or change proposals to be individually considered for approval or rejection, and also compared objectively with other projects or options. In the SALVO case, this stage also involves sensitivity-testing, to identify the degree of confidence in these conclusions, and identify any assumptions that need to be investigated further before a decision is made.

Putting these elements together with range-estimating skills and rapid 'what if?' calculations, we find that a) the analysis team focusses on the factors that matter in the decision (reducing the time wasted in discussion of peripheral and non-critical aspects) and b) the resulting conclusions have a much higher confidence and general acceptance.

> **Example**: In one case, over 400 projects where evaluated by just two people in 3 weeks, showed immediate savings of over £2.5 million in re-targeting of priorities. In another (one of the biggest oil refineries in the world), *all* change proposals were screened in this way, reducing the average evaluation time from 8 man-hours per project to just 30 man-minutes, while also achieving greater consistency and auditability.

5.4.2.2 Decision-making criteria

For these simple Yes/No decisions, the approval criterion needs to be clearly understood. The ISO 55001 standard for Asset Management explicitly also requires documented 'decision-making criteria' to be part of any competent management system. But there are several different ways of calculating and presenting the value-for-money attractiveness of projects or one-off changes. These range from the simple concept of a Payback Period, to more sophisticated financial indicators such as the Internal Rate of Return (IRR) or Profitability Index (PI) (see Figure 32). The SALVO process does not insist on any particular method, since each has advantages and disadvantages. However it is valuable to know these strengths and limitations in selecting the criterion to be used in the organisation.

		Best	Likely	Worst	
Discounted payback period		12	15	25	Months
NPV	£	151000(	764000	283000	
IRR		1040	353	96.5	%
PI		72.1	33	10.7	

Figure 32. Ranges of results with potential decision criteria

Payback Period is a simple arithmetic calculation of how long it will take for benefits to recover the costs of the project/change. So a $5,000 investment, yielding a risk reduction, or performance improvement, of $1,000/year will take 5 years to 'pay back' the costs.   The method is extremely easy to understand, and is valuable for quick screening of ideas and comparison between options. Indeed it is probably the most useful method for engaging the workforce in the basics of cost/benefit appraisal as part of any continual improvement or suggestion scheme.

However the Payback Period only considers benefits up to the 'breakeven' point. It does not consider or help in scaling the added-value benefits beyond this point, so it could not distinguish between, say a $5,000 project yielding $1,000/year benefits, and a $20,000 project, yielding $4,000/year benefits: both have a 5-year Payback Period, but the *ongoing* benefits (beyond the breakeven point) of the bigger project are 4 times those of the smaller one.

Discounted **Payback Period**. This is a refinement of the simple arithmetic payback calculation – it takes account of the time delay between incurring the costs of a change and receiving of the benefits. This introduces the concept of *discounted cashflow*, whereby future benefits are 'discounted' down into today's equivalent value (Present Day Value or PV).   The mechanism for such discounting is very simple: it reduces each future cashflow (in our case, risk, performance or financial benefit) by a 'discount factor' for each year into the future we have to await it.

Example: If the discount factor is 10%/year, the discounted payback point for a $5,000 investment is nearly 7 years (compared to 5 years for undiscounted benefits): see Table 5.

Year	Undiscounted Benefit $/year	Cumulative Benefit ($)	Discounted PV $/year	Cumulative (PV $)
1	1000	1000	1000	1000
2	1000	2000	900	1900
3	1000	3000	810	2710
4	1000	4000	729	3439
5	1000	5000	656	4095
6	1000	6000	590	4685
7	1000	7000	531	5217

Table 5: Discounted Payback Period

The choice of an appropriate discount factor can have a big impact on project approvals and decision-making. The cumulative effects of 10%/year would change the Payback Period from 5 years to nearly 7 years (see Table 5). This discount factor therefore needs to be determined carefully, and needs to reflect the organisation's financial position: it reflects the state of borrowing or cash-rich position of the organisation's balance sheet, and what alternative uses for money exist (e.g. earning interest in the bank, or paying off a debt, or investing in alternative business ventures). In most organisations a discount rate is therefore defined by the finance department, either as a figure to be used universally or, sometimes, with specific ranges of applicability (different rules may apply for very large investments, or for certain classes of project or types of benefit).

Net Present Value (NPV) is a further improvement in the flexibility and comprehensiveness of decision-making criteria, and is widely used in project or investment evaluations. Unlike Payback Period, or even Discounted Payback Period, NPV considers ongoing benefits beyond the 'break-even' point. In fact it can be used with any horizon of benefits, with appropriate discounting of their future impact back to today's equivalent values. It is therefore a measure of the 'total value' obtained from a combination of costs and benefits over a chosen period (See Figure 33). A positive value indicates that the benefits are greater than the costs, and the size of the positive value indicates, in present day financial terms, *how much* the benefits exceed the costs, having already taking into account the effect of having to wait for these benefits.

$$NPV = A + M_1 + \sum_{i=2}^{n} p^{i-1} M_i - p^n S_n$$

A = Cost of project or change
M_i = Future cashflow (e.g. benefits) in year **i**
S_n = Recoverable value/cashflow at horizon **n**
r = Annual discount rate
p = 1/(1+r) = the discount factor

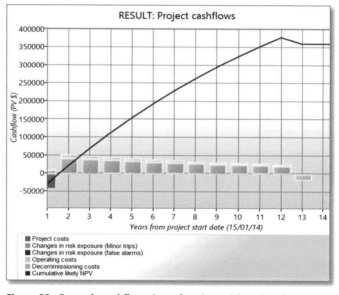

Figure 33. Example cashflow view of project with various impacts

NPV also has limitations, however. It requires a chosen horizon over which the benefits can be calculated – and not all changes or projects will have the same duration of resulting benefits. To address this weakness, most organisations select an evaluation horizon of, say, 20 years or more. This is sufficiently long-term to include the majority of benefits, as the discounting process renders any further benefits beyond this point to be very marginal in today's equivalent value. Alternatively, an NPV for an 'infinite' horizon can be calculated – this presumes ongoing benefits without an artificial limit, allowing a wider range of options to be evaluated and compared for Net Present Value, even if they represent very long timescale benefits indeed. However this does not work well for comparing projects with constrained benefit periods alongside projects that have indefinite or unconstrained/ongoing benefits. In particular it is a poor evaluation method for decisions that affect asset life cycles, since the options might each have a different achievable benefits horizon (asset life). Fortunately there is a solution for this – the equivalent annualized value of all the cashflows.

Equivalent Annual Cost (EAC) turns the NPV into an annualized amount, taking the case-by-case period of benefits into account. The resulting figure is the present day value which, if incurred (or received) every year in perpetuity, *would be the same as the NPV over the relevant horizon*. The important thing about EAC is that it irons out the problems of different NPV horizons or benefit periods – so it is a measure that can be used to directly compare cheaper, short-lived projects with higher cost but longer benefit cases. And it is ideal for evaluating different asset life cycles and projects that affect life cycles. We will be using EAC, therefore, in other storyboards for other asset management interventions, where benefits are not simple *levels* of cost, risk or performance change but also have a timing and sustainability implication.

$$EAC = \frac{r\left\{A + M_1 + \sum_{i=2}^{n} p^{i-1}M_i - p^n S_n\right\}}{1 - p^n}$$

A = Cost of project or change
M_i = Future cashflow (e.g. benefits) in year i
S_n = Recoverable value/cashflow at horizon n
r = Annual discount rate
p = 1/(1+r) = the discount factor

Internal Rate of Return (IRR) is another measure of project attractiveness, popular with finance departments. In concept it represents the percentage return on investment that the proposed change delivers. But it does this in a roundabout way – it is the rate at which future benefits have to be discounted before the total NPV becomes exactly neutral (costs equate to the benefits). This finds the tipping point – if the cost of capital (or yields from alternative usage of the money) is bigger than this percentage then, in comparison, this project is not attractive. So IRR is primarily useful as a *comparative* indicator, for when a project or improvement proposal is competing for funds with other projects or with external investment/savings/debt repayment opportunities. Nevertheless it is a good measure of the intrinsic value of a proposed action – provided the 'required IRR' value for decision approval is kept up to date with the changing commercial environment. IRR is also quite difficult to calculate: the following equation has to be solved to find the discount rate (IRR) that forces the NPV to have zero value:

$$NPV = 0 = P_0 + P_1/(1+IRR) + P_2/(1+IRR)_2 + P_3/(1+IRR)_3 + \ldots + P_n/(1+IRR)_n$$

where P_0, P_1, ... P_n are the cashflows in periods 1, 2, ... n.

Finally, the **Profitability Index (PI)** (sometimes called a Financing or Finance Indicator or Index) is sometimes considered the best value-for-money criterion. This is simply the NPV divided by the up-front cost of the project, so it represents the earning power for the at-risk investment amount. It provides some compensation for the fact that big projects, yielding big benefits, are not the same value proposition as a small project with proportionately smaller benefits even if their NPV values are equivalent. And, if there is a range of project sizes to be considered, then only investing in the biggest one represents 'all eggs in the same basket', whereas spending the same amount of money on several smaller ones instead provides greater flexibility and diversification security. PI is therefore one of the most useful indicators for managing a projects portfolio, particularly if it includes a wide range of project sizes.

$$PI = NPV/project\ cost$$

5.4.2.3   Putting a price on Compliance or Intangibles

Most of the evaluation discipline has involved quantification of the costs and benefits, considering the various Shamrock dimensions of potential business impact.   The Compliance and Shine dimensions, however, are best handled once the rest of the evaluation process is complete.   In fact we need the results of an objective cost/benefit/risk evaluation (*without* taking the Compliance obligations or Shine/intangibles into account) before we can consider how much influence these additional factors should have upon the decision.   The technique that SALVO has developed is to calculate the inferred *premium paid* for these factors: this is the amount of project cost that is not self-funding by tangible or quantified benefits.

> **For example**, if a project costs £10,000 and will result in £2,000/year of cost/risk/performance benefits, and the normal decision criterion is that projects are approved if they have a payback period of 24 months or less, then this project is not going to be approved.   If there are additional Shine benefits, such as health and safety or environmental benefits, client satisfaction or staff morale, over and above the quantified benefits, then these intangibles would have to be valuable enough to swing the No decision into a Yes.   There are £2,000/year of tangible benefits so, in the required 2 years, £4,000 of the project cost has been recovered, leaving **£6,000 still unjustified**, *so the Shine benefits would have to be worth at least this amount for the project to be approved.*

Any absolute obligations to implement a project create a Compliance motivation, over and above any quantified risk, performance, cost or even Shine considerations.   Like the evaluation of the Shine significance, the SALVO method derives a '*Premium paid for Compliance'* by calculating the shortfall in business justification for the investment or change.   If the project does not deliver enough tangible benefits to be self-funding, then the compliance obligation is the deciding factor – and the proportion of the benefits that are 'real' (i.e. the smallness of the premium paid for such compliance) provides an excellent criterion for prioritizing the project's implementation, especially if there are several mandatory projects competing for limited resources.

This method for quantifying the influence of Shine and Compliance factors is extremely powerful and flexible. It encourages much greater transparency and consistency in the treatment of intangibles such as reputation, morale and societal responsibility, and in the logical handling of non-negotiable project commitments (indeed, if the premium paid for compliance is revealed as very large, it may be worth negotiating!).

5.4.2.4   Use of scenarios

A variant of this Project/Change Evaluation process is the choice between alternative ways of solving the same problem. This is handled by the SALVO process (and DST software) by the use of Scenarios and an example is shown in Figure 34 below. Any decision may have multiple scenarios explored and compared before a final choice is made. And the scenarios might reflect all sorts of different assumptions, options or variants. For example, a potential procedure change might be evaluated with different assumptions about the scope of its implementation (and therefore costs and effects). Or a modification project might have different technical specification options, vendor options, logistics assumptions, configurations etc. Any or all of these could be represented by simply copying the original 'Base Case' evaluation, and editing the descriptive and quantified assumptions to reflect the differences. In the final 'decision-making' stage of the storyboard, these scenarios can be directly compared and the best value solution selected (Figure 34).

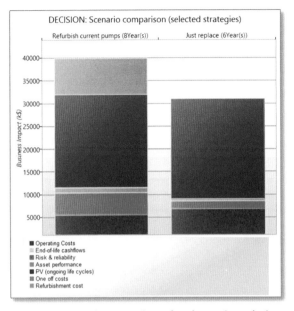

Figure 34. Scenario comparisons for alternative solutions

Note, however, that scenarios should not be confused with data sensitivity testing. If the differences in assumption are just alternative views about the same situation (i.e. there is uncertainty), you should enter this as data uncertainty (range estimates) to discover if this has any impact on the decision. Keep any data uncertainty explorations *within* the scenario to avoid confusion.

5.4.2.5 Decision authority levels

For smaller projects and change proposals, the decision-making process and allocation of budget or resources can be very different to that of major investments. Some organisations delegate a certain amount of decision freedom and budgets to departmental or functional improvement areas - within which discrete project ideas can be evaluated and approved, or rejected without further reference to the bigger picture. This can lead to problems, when people recognise that subdividing a project into smaller packages can get commitment more easily than presenting a proper, total programme proposal. So any difference in the storyboard for evaluating small projects to that of evaluating larger commitments must incorporate safeguards and escalation criteria, whereby dependencies or linkages between projects are identified, or the potential impact of a small project could warrant greater scrutiny even if the immediate cost implications are below the authorisation threshold. The SALVO process has recommended a combination of two 'escalation criteria' for this (note that most organisations only consider the first of these in setting decision authorisation levels):

a)   cost of the project/change OR

b)   business impact of the project/change, most easily represented by the level of cost/risk/performance that is being addressed.

This pair of criteria should typically be used to create three bands of decision authorization:

- **Minor** projects, with delegated authority for projects/changes, whose direct cost is below a defined low cost amount **AND** which are addressing a low impact issue (below a defined level). *e.g. Below £10k cost AND below £5k/year business impact.*

- **Normal**/formal project approval required, with decision validation and endorsement by affected stakeholders, for projects/changes in a defined cost range **AND** having an impact between defined low and high limits. *e.g. Between £10k and £1M cost AND between £5k/year and £500k/year business impact.*

- **Major** investment projects, with special case consideration at fully-escalated authority levels, for those investments above a high cost threshold **OR** which have potential impact above a specified level. *e.g. Above £1M cost OR above £500k/year business impact.*

Note that **Major** projects will very rarely be approved for implementation without reference to other projects and other potential uses of the money or resources. Any significant commitment to change or investment must be reviewed at the **portfolio** level as well, at which point the full range of activities and projects are considered for their *combined* need for funding and resourcing. This is will be handled in Step 6 of SALVO.

However if there is a significant number **minor** and **normal** projects to consider, then these too might be reviewed, not just individually for a Yes/No decision, but as a ranked portfolio, to ensure that the best value projects receive the available funds, resources and priority implementation. The SALVO toolbox (DST Asset Strategy Evaluators) has specific facilities for this, in the form of Batch evaluation, ranking criteria, reporting and handling of budget constraints - see Figure 35, showing which mandatory projects (blue) and the best value projects (green) fit within a budget, while poorer value projects (red) are identified as not affordable.

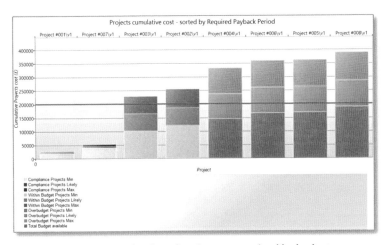

Figure 35. Evaluation of projects constrained by budget

5.4.3 Evaluating inspections

The options that involve finding something out (usually asset condition) need a different cost/benefit appraisal. Inspections are motivated by the value of improved information that is obtained – and what that information, in turn, is used for.

For example, the problem identified in SALVO Step 2 might have been a business risk associated with unknown asset condition, and the potential actions (identified in SALVO Step 3) might include a condition assessment. We now need to evaluate the cost/benefit of such an assessment, taking account of direct and indirect costs (if the assets need to be shut down for the inspection), any risks *introduced* by the inspection, and the resulting discovery possibilities, such as improved prediction and prevention, or discovery and correction, of asset failures. And inspections are often subject to regulatory requirements, so compliance may be a motive, or there may be 'Shine' benefits of greater confidence for internal and external stakeholders.

The SALVO process splits the inspection evaluations into four different storyboards for the relevant questions that must be asked and the cost/benefit calculations that are necessary:

- **Failure finding** inspections, such as functional testing, to discover existing but hidden failure modes. These are characteristic of safety protection systems and stand-by equipment, whose function is only needed occasionally.

- **Predictive** inspections (sometimes called **Condition Monitoring, Condition-based Maintenance** or **Predictive Maintenance**). These address the wide range of health assessment options, ranging from one-off surveys to periodic inspections or measures to continuous, on-line monitoring with sophisticated multi-parameter diagnostics and alarms. For cost/benefit evaluation, the predictive inspection cases fall into three categories:

    o **One-off** inspections or condition assessments
    o **Periodic** inspections or condition monitoring
    o **Continuous** condition monitoring

5.4.3.1   Failure finding and functional testing

The determination of testing intervals has been modelled extensively in high criticality environments, such as nuclear, petrochemical and aviation sectors. However, this has mostly been done from the pure integrity management viewpoint, often considering the economics at only a superficial, rule-based level. The SALVO methods have used the relevant risk and reliability engineering mathematics but have also incorporated the costs of the testing, possible risks introduced by the testing and, even if the primary objective is to discover existing (hidden) failures, there are sometimes secondary, preventive maintenance benefits from intrusive inspections or testing (such as the functional testing of electrical switchgear which also moves the grease around, reducing the risk of subsequent 'stiction' failures).

Information needed to determine an optimal **testing strategy** includes:
- Cost of the testing: direct costs, downtime impact (which may itself represent a period of risk exposure), other penalties and timing alignment opportunities.
- Risk of failure due to the test, leaving the asset in a failed state following the test.
- Inherent failure rate: the accumulating risk of asset being in an unrevealed failed state (this is what the test is trying to reveal).
- Beneficial effects of testing upon subsequent failure rate: degree of risk reduction and duration of such reduced risk.
- Testing success rate: confidence level in the testing method.
- Operational demand: the frequency of occasions at which the asset is required to perform its designed function.
- Consequences of failure on demand: direct and indirect impact of asset not performing its function when required to do so. This may include an increased dependency on further layers of protection system (an 'escalation risk').
- Constraints on the strategy, such as mandatory inspection intervals, or maximum tolerable event probabilities.
- Shine factors and preferences for increased confidence or 'sleep easy at night' comfort.

The SALVO storyboard and capture of this information (or range-estimates for it) is shown in Figure 36.

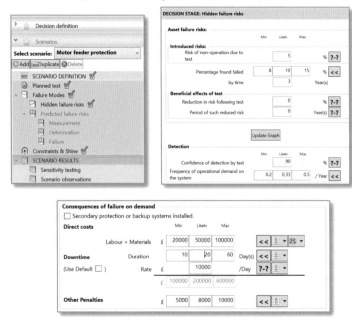

Figure 36. Storyboard and factors to consider in optimizing test intervals

Calculating the net risk exposures and costs of different testing intervals is non-trivial but handled instantly in the DST Inspection Evaluator, so that 'What if?' studies and sensitivity testing become practical.

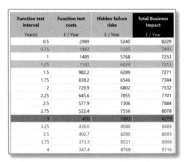
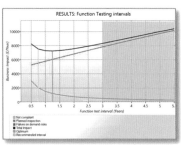

Figure 37. Optimized testing interval: results and compliance limits

Although the optimum for 'most likely' assumptions is 15 monthly testing (light green highlight in Figure 37), the vulnerability to uncertain data means that a 9-monthly test is a better strategy (darker green). This strategy is the least vulnerable to the data error coming from all the range-estimates that have been included. If the recommended (9-monthly) strategy is implemented, the 'cost of uncertainty' (worst impact of error due to the poor data quality) is £1,070/year (Figure 38).

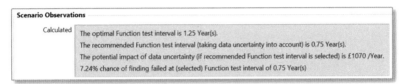

Figure 38. Auto-generated observations from the analysis

Finally, as hidden failures and function testing are often associated with safety and integrity management, it is particularly important to see the residual risk view of the different testing strategies. This provides the assurance of testing effectiveness, irrespective of the economics involved (see Figure 39 and 'FAILURE RISKS' section of Figure 40).

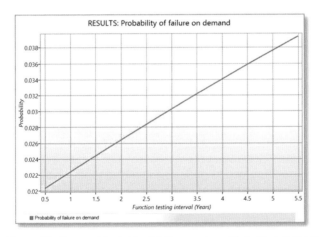

Figure 39. How residual risk of failure varies with testing strategy

Results details		Current	Optimum	Constrained	Recommended	Selected	
Function test interval		3	1.25	1.25	0.75	0.75	Year(s)
BUSINESS IMPACT							
Total Business Impact	£	8280	7210	7210	7490	7490	/ Year
Total Direct Costs (Materials & Labour)	£	1990	2350	2350	3050	3050	/ Year
Total Penalty Costs	£	6290	4860	4860	4440	4440	/ Year
Total Downtime Costs	£	6050	4680	4680	4270	4270	/ Year
PLANNED Function test							
Function test Direct Costs (Materials & Labour)	£	475	1180	1180	1980	1980	/ Year
Function test Penalty Costs	£	0.792	1.969	1.969	3.306	3.306	/ Year
Function test Downtime Costs	£	476	1180	1180	1990	1990	/ Year
Function test Downtime	Day(s)	1.397	2.437	2.437	3.732	3.732	/ Year
FAILURE RISKS							
Hidden failure risks							
Probability of finding failed		0.122	0.084	0.084	0.072	0.072	
Fractional dead time		9.21	7.088	7.088	6.468	6.468	%
Probability of failure on demand		0.03	0.023	0.023	0.021	0.021	
Failures on demand direct costs	£	1510	1170	1170	1070	1070	/ Year
Failures on demand penalty costs	£	6290	4860	4860	4440	4440	/ Year
Failures on demand downtime costs	£	6050	4670	4670	4270	4270	/ Year

Figure 40. Detailed cost and risk implications of different strategies

5.4.3.2 Inspection to predict and prevent failure

Different methods of cost/benefit evaluation are needed for one-off condition assessments, for periodic condition or performance inspections and for continual or on-line condition monitoring.

5.4.3.3 One-off condition assessments

In the first case, a single condition assessment activity can be handled much like any other one-off task: by estimating of the levels of cost, risk and performance if a) nothing is done and b) once the assessment has occurred (i.e. the change in level of knowledge that will result). It takes a little visualising, but the 'payback' for the costs of such an inspection must be sufficient to justify the task, in the same way as any other activity (Project/Change Evaluation process in section 5.4.4).

In the SALVO approach, there is also sometimes a way of calculating 'up front' the value of acquiring this additional asset condition information. At the time of writing nobody has fully explored this yet, but the ability to calculate a 'cost of uncertainty' in other decision types (such as 'when should I replace the asset?') has been used as a direct measure of the potential value of better information. If the cost of an inspection or data improvement activity is less than the 'cost of uncertainty' (decision vulnerability due to uncertain assumptions), then the data collection is worthwhile.

5.4.3.4   Periodic condition monitoring inspections

Regular inspections need to be justified on the basis of their ability to provide early warning of the need to intervene and prevent asset failure. They either look for evidence that a degradation mechanism has started or they monitor its progress so that a more intrusive maintenance activity (or asset renewal) can occur at the right point.   In maintenance strategy literature, this is often represented by a 'P-F curve', based on the concept that degradation can be identified and monitored between a Potential failure point ('P': the detectable onset of the failure mechanism) and the Functional failure point ('F': the point at which the asset fails to perform its required function, which may or may not be manifested as mechanical breakdown or catastrophic loss).   In conventional explanation, however, the P and F points are assumed to be known and reasonably consistent (see Figure 41). In real life this is rarely true.

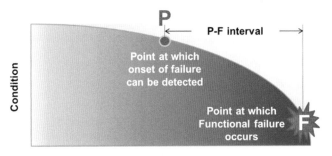

Figure 41. P-F curve

Cost/benefit evaluation of the inspections therefore requires us to explore uncertainty in both the 'P' and 'F' points, and the variability in deterioration rates that might occur between these points. We also have to consider the consequences of possible discoveries (such as a short-notice corrective action if the degradation has gone beyond a permissible limit), or of being 'too late' (asset functional failure). We need to consider the inspection costs, of course, along with any risks we might introduce by performing the inspection, and any constraints (such as mandatory inspection obligations) or Shine factors (of improved confidence and credibility).

Information needed to evaluate the cost/benefit and optimal timing of **predictive/preventive inspections** includes:

- Cost of the inspection: direct costs, downtime impact (which may itself represent a period of risk exposure), other penalties and timing alignment opportunities.
- Sample size, number of assets or sources of risk inspected by the task.
- Measurement units and measurement accuracy: these range from a simple visual 'condition grade' scale to an instrumented measurement, with highly varied calibration/tolerances.
- Threshold of detectable onset of deterioration (the Potential failure or 'P' point in a P-F curve), and the uncertainty in this point.
- If onset is not inevitable (i.e. it requires some initiating event, such as shock loading of a bearing, or penetration of a paint or other protective coating), we need to estimate the background frequency of the initiating events.
- Degradation rates and their variability: this may be a pattern of observed data (if available), or range-estimated forecasts. If Risk Based Inspection (RBI) studies have been performed, this pattern is represented by calculated average rates and examples of extreme rates.
- Permissible limits (such as a 'corrosion allowance'): if inspection discovers deterioration beyond this point, costs and downtime may be required to repair the asset prior to functional failure.
- Corrective costs, penalty costs and consequences of discovering deterioration beyond the permissible limit.
- The point of Functional failure ('F' point in a P-F curve): either as a range-estimate the degradation point at which failure would occur,

or an inferred risk zone obtained by extrapolating from the 'permissible limit', assuming a design safety factor

- Consequences of functional failure: direct costs, downtime impact and penalty costs, including any escalation risks and secondary consequences.
- Constraints on the strategy, such as mandatory inspection intervals, or maximum tolerable event probabilities.
- Shine factors and preferences for increased confidence or 'sleep easy at night' comfort.

The DST Inspection Evaluator module provides a corresponding storyboard and quantification methods for data entry or range-estimating (Figure 40).

Example: *wall thickness monitoring of corroding pipework.*

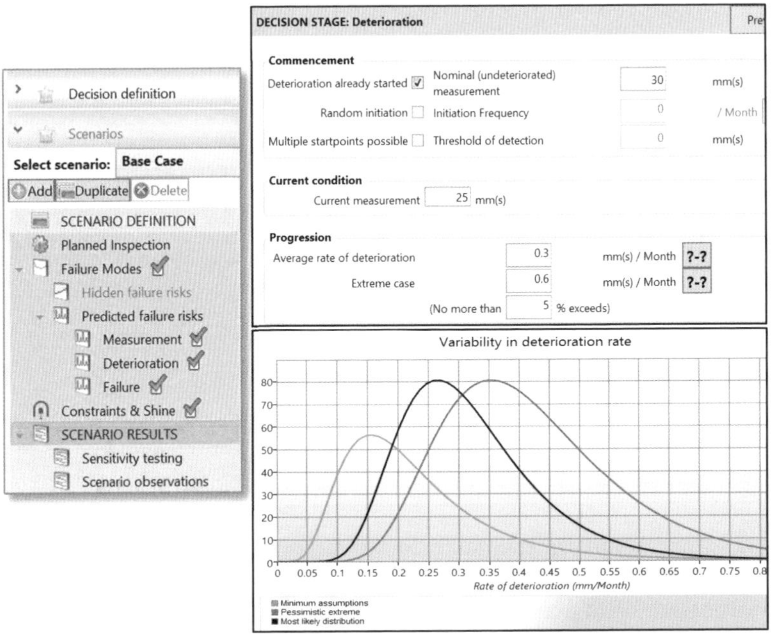

Figure 42. Storyboard and information capture for predictive inspections

When the cost of the inspection is added, and the typically uncertain zone of asset failure, DST Inspection Evaluator calculates the relationship between inspection frequency and the risks of a) discovering we are already beyond the permissible limit, and therefore needing to incur a corrective cost, and b) asset functional failure, with its costs and consequences (see Figure 43).

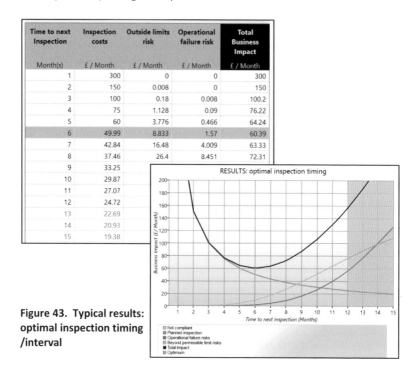

Time to next Inspection	Inspection costs	Outside limits risk	Operational failure risk	Total Business Impact
Month(s)	£ / Month	£ / Month	£ / Month	£ / Month
1	300	0	0	300
2	150	0.008	0	150
3	100	0.18	0.008	100.2
4	75	1.128	0.09	76.22
5	60	3.776	0.466	64.24
6	49.99	8.833	1.57	60.39
7	42.84	16.48	4.009	63.33
8	37.46	26.4	8.451	72.31
9	33.25			
10	29.87			
11	27.07			
12	24.72			
13	22.69			
14	20.93			
15	19.38			

RESULTS: optimal inspection timing

Business Impact (£ / Month)

Time to next Inspection (Months)

Not compliant
Planned inspection
Operational failure risks
Beyond permissible limit risks
Total Impact
Optimum

Figure 43. Typical results: optimal inspection timing /interval

By incorporating uncertainty into the estimates, the calculation reveals that 'fuzzy' P-F intervals (uncertain detection point, uncertain failure point and uncertain degradation rates), can still help us to identify and demonstrate an optimal or recommended inspection timing (see Figure 44). This is equally applicable to visual condition surveys, vibration monitoring, corrosion monitoring, temperature and pressure monitoring and periodic asset performance checks.

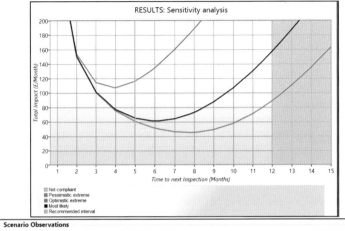

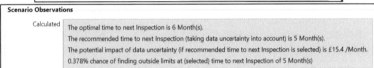

Figure 44. Sensitivity testing and selection of best value strategy

In the case of periodic condition inspections, there is also a further refinement in SALVO Step 4. These decisions can be iterative, since the findings of one inspection can be used directly to update the 'current' level of deterioration to re-evaluate when next to inspect. This is why DST Inspection Evaluator presents results as 'Time to next inspection' rather than assume ongoing consistent intervals. If the latest reading shows advanced deterioration, then the optimal time to re-inspect will be sooner. As we get closer to the cliff edge, we should be monitoring more and more frequently. So the SALVO optimization process is a dynamic one, with a feedback loop from each measurement acting as an updated input to the determination of next occasion.

5.4.3.5 Continuous or on-line condition monitoring

When the failure mechanism has a very short development period (P-F interval) and/or the failure consequences are particularly large, it may be worthwhile to establish a continuous or on-line monitoring system. And this does not always involve installing expensive instrumentation systems: we must remember that suitably trained equipment operators can also be very effective, flexible and sensitive detectors of change or warning signs.

Nevertheless, the acquisition, installation (or operator training) and ongoing maintenance of the monitoring system itself needs to be evaluated and justified. The methods of this evaluation, however, depend upon what is the alternative to the proposed monitoring method. If we are simply comparing on-line monitoring with a run-to-failure alternative, then the evaluation is a fairly simple with/without comparison to determine the risk differences in return for any capital investment and ongoing operating costs (and risks of initiating 'false alarms).

If, on the other hand, *some* of the failures could have been prevented by a fixed-interval preventive maintenance routine, and the on-line/continuous condition monitoring is proposed as a more sensitive and effective way of preventing failures, then the evaluation should be a comparative one – based on the anticipated increase in success (preventive) rate of condition-based interventions compared to the fixed-interval regime.

The information needed for evaluating a **continuous condition monitoring** option includes:

- Procurement, installation and commissioning costs for the monitoring system, including training and procedures for responding to the resulting 'alarm bells'.
- Ongoing operating costs of the system.
- Failure modes that the system can detect.
- For each failure mode, background frequency of occurrence, % detectable in the P-F stage (i.e. with adequate leadtime to react and pre-empt functional failure).
- Failure rate of the monitoring system itself (% of potential/ diagnosable warnings missed).
- False alarm rate (triggering inappropriate response and cost)
- Response time to a diagnosed warning condition (compared to P-F interval).
- Range/variability in the response time and the P-F interval

- Costs and consequences of successful corrective action responding to an alarm condition.
- Costs and consequences of functional failure (either without the monitoring system, or through failure of the monitoring system to provide adequate preventive warning).

The evaluation method for establishing a continuous monitoring system is a 'step-change' (with/without the system) rather than an interval evaluation, so it follows the storyboard of a Project/Change Evaluation as described in section 5.4.2).

Example: installing an on-line monitoring system

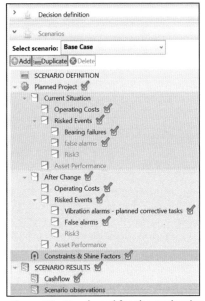

Figure 45. Storyboard for the evaluation

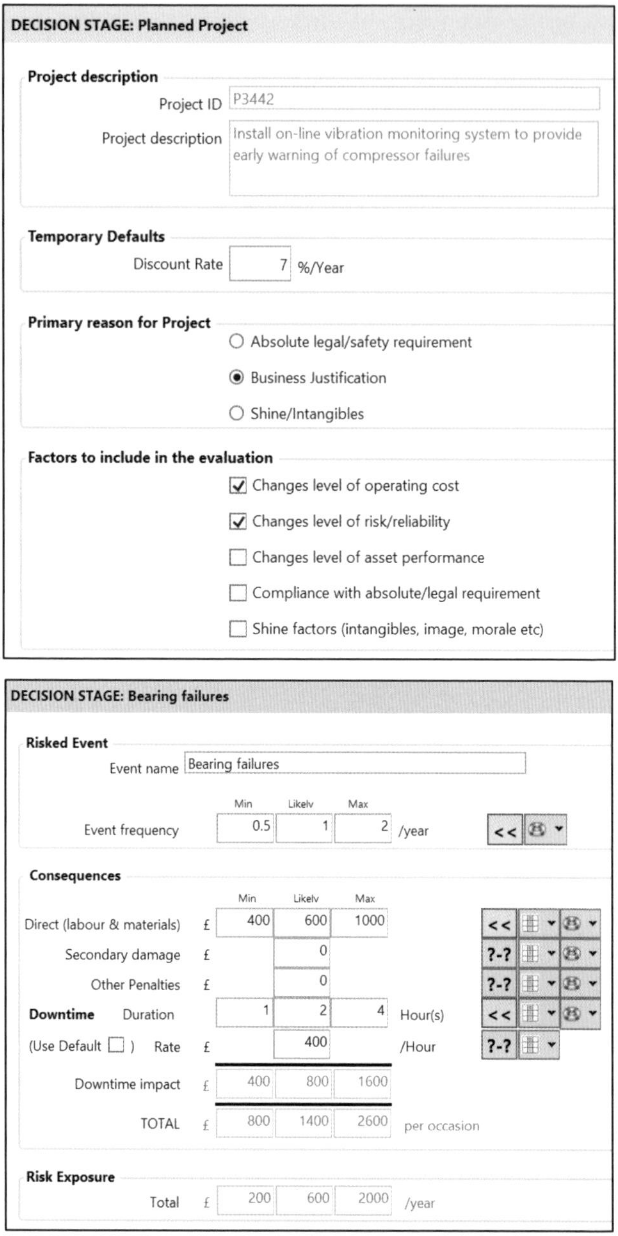

DECISION STAGE: Planned Project

Project description

Project ID P3442

Project description Install on-line vibration monitoring system to provide early warning of compressor failures

Temporary Defaults

Discount Rate 7 %/Year

Primary reason for Project

○ Absolute legal/safety requirement

◉ Business Justification

○ Shine/Intangibles

Factors to include in the evaluation

☑ Changes level of operating cost

☑ Changes level of risk/reliability

☐ Changes level of asset performance

☐ Compliance with absolute/legal requirement

☐ Shine factors (intangibles, image, morale etc)

DECISION STAGE: Bearing failures

Risked Event

Event name Bearing failures

	Min	Likely	Max	
Event frequency	0.5	1	2	/year

Consequences

		Min	Likely	Max	
Direct (labour & materials)	£	400	600	1000	
Secondary damage	£	0			
Other Penalties	£	0			
Downtime Duration		1	2	4	Hour(s)
(Use Default ☐) Rate	£	400			/Hour
Downtime impact	£	400	800	1600	
TOTAL	£	800	1400	2600	per occasion

Risk Exposure

		Min	Likely	Max	
Total	£	200	600	2000	/year

Figure 46. Decision set-up & quantifying failure risks with *no system installed*

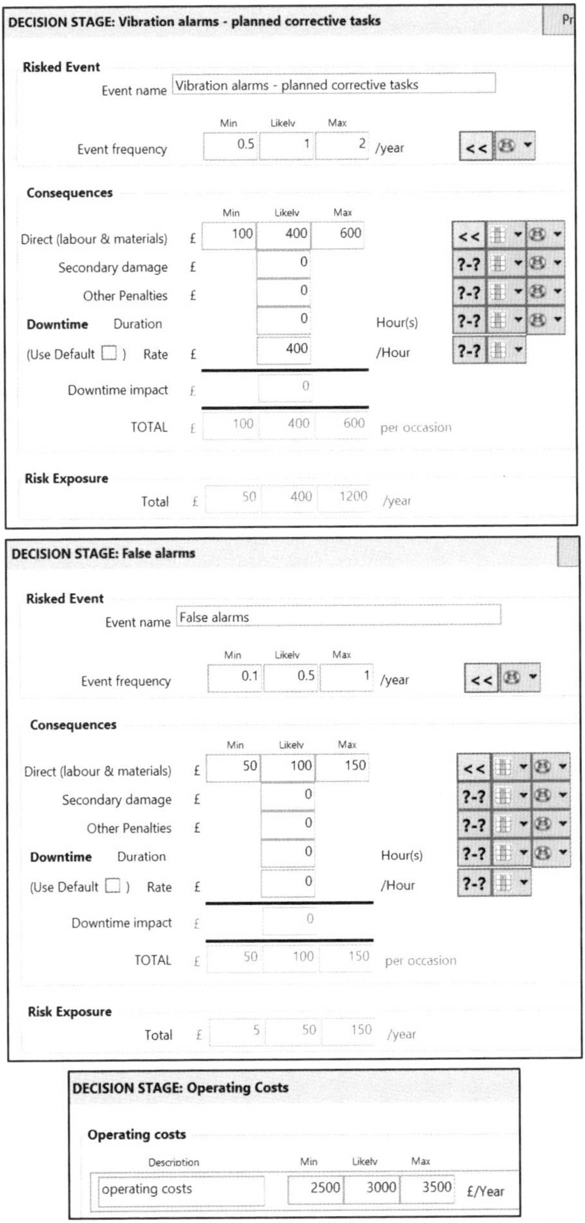

DECISION STAGE: Vibration alarms - planned corrective tasks

Risked Event

Event name: Vibration alarms - planned corrective tasks

	Min	Likely	Max	
Event frequency	0.5	1	2	/year

Consequences

		Min	Likely	Max	
Direct (labour & materials)	£	100	400	600	
Secondary damage	£		0		
Other Penalties	£		0		
Downtime Duration			0		Hour(s)
(Use Default ☐) Rate	£		400		/Hour
Downtime impact	£		0		
TOTAL	£	100	400	600	per occasion

Risk Exposure

Total	£	50	400	1200	/year

DECISION STAGE: False alarms

Risked Event

Event name: False alarms

	Min	Likely	Max	
Event frequency	0.1	0.5	1	/year

Consequences

		Min	Likely	Max	
Direct (labour & materials)	£	50	100	150	
Secondary damage	£		0		
Other Penalties	£		0		
Downtime Duration			0		Hour(s)
(Use Default ☐) Rate	£		0		/Hour
Downtime impact	£		0		
TOTAL	£	50	100	150	per occasion

Risk Exposure

Total	£	5	50	150	/year

DECISION STAGE: Operating Costs

Operating costs

Description	Min	Likely	Max	
operating costs	2500	3000	3500	£/Year

Figure 47. *With system installed*: residual failure risks, plus <u>new</u> risks & costs

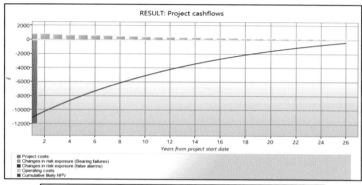

Figure 48. Results showing that, in this case, the payback
period is not good enough (35 months, even in optimistic case)

5.4.4   Planned maintenance evaluations

The evaluation of planned maintenance (PM) options is a very big and diverse subject in its own right. It covers three main areas of motivation and therefore cost/benefit appraisal:

- prevention (preventive maintenance),
- correction (planned corrective maintenance, recovering losses of performance or operating cost/efficiency)
- asset life-extension (*slowing* the processes of deterioration).

In addition to these, we often encounter mandatory obligations (Compliance) and perception impacts or intangibles (Shine factors). Indeed, a significant planned maintenance task, such as a compressor overhaul, or a building refurbishment, can include effects on all dimensions of the Shamrock diagram, with all stakeholder interests being affected to some degree.   Accordingly, the storyboard for these evaluations is highly variable, ranging from a simple PM versus Run-To-Failure up to a multi-page, multi-dimension optimization of workscope, performance patterns, multiple risk patterns, lifespan effects, compliance and shine factors. The following sections provide examples of discrete cases, but the SALVO methodology applies equally well to those where all elements are interacting simultaneously.

5.4.4.1 Preventive maintenance

Information needed to evaluate a **preventive maintenance** task:
- Planned maintenance scope, which may vary with the condition found (i.e. a distribution of costs) and/or with time since last performed (i.e. a trend, with the scope growing at longer intervals due to the accumulated damage and 'corrective' tasks included).
- Risks introduced by the PM task; likelihood, period of likely discovery, costs and consequences (including any recoverable costs if warranty applies).
- Failure modes and the necessary corrective repair tasks that would occur (including the degree of 'resetting the clock' for subsequent deterioration, risks and PM urgency).
- For each 'clock resetting' failure mode, the probability patterns (reducing, random and/or increasing risk) and uncertainties in the

patterns. **Note**: SALVO quantification methods for 'Survival Curves' greatly improve our ability to quantify such patterns.

- For 'Patch-and-Continue' failure modes, the frequency of such events in relation to time since last PM, and the uncertainty in this pattern.

- For all failure modes, the costs and consequences of failure, which (like PM) may vary not just in uncertainty ranges, but as a distribution of outcomes, or as a trend (if they occur later, they may tend to be larger).

- Constraints: are there any mandatory requirements applicable to the task (e.g. interval or maximum tolerable failure risk)?

- Opportunities: is there a periodic access opportunity or advantage of aligning the PM interval with other activities (e.g. shutdowns or remote site visits).

- Shine factors: are there any morale, reputation, image or other intangible impacts of the PM versus Run-to-failure decision?

The planned versus unplanned decision is conceptually fairly simple but, in mathematical terms, extremely complex – particularly if the planned activity introduces some element of risk itself, or there is more than one failure mode involved, or the corrective maintenance response to a failure does not fully 'reset the clock' for subsequent planned activities.

The SALVO methods incorporate the full depth of Renewal Theory and Reliability Engineering calculations, and further extend these to evaluate the mutual 'censoring' effects of one failure mode upon the exposure to another (and *vice versa*). For example, if a pump has a risk of foreign object damage as well as seal degradation and impeller wear, then the frequency of damage by the foreign objects (and consequent corrective maintenance) may change the proportion of pumps whose seals reach the point of failure, or bearings wear out. Similarly, the failure of bearings will normally result in seals being changed during the repair – so the frequency of bearing failures affects the risks of seal failures.

This is not a guidebook on reliability engineering, but some basic concepts need to be understood in order to appreciate what has to be 'under the skin' in the modelling and optimization of preventive maintenance tasks and their intervals. Many current commercial tools are claiming to 'optimize' planned maintenance but only consider a simplified trade-off between [PM cost] and [probability x consequence of a single asset failure mode]. Real life tends to have more complexity and risk interdependencies.

5.4.4.2 Quantifying patterns of risk

The underlying assumption in any PM justification is that risk of failure would increase if the PM were not performed or left 'too late'. In other words, the risks are increasing with time or asset usage. Quantifying the *rate of increase in risk* is very hard, however, particularly in the absence of sufficient detailed and consistent failure history. Even the methods introduced for capturing expert opinion (such as the Sherlock Holmes method explained in section 2.3.2) struggle to visualise "if the asset is left, say 12 months longer, how much higher would the risk-per-day be?". Fortunately, the MACRO project addressed this issue effectively, by developing an indirect quantification method that people are much more comfortable with for quantifying and sharing their knowledge. This is the Survival Curve: the cumulative effect of failure risks, expressed as the proportion of occasions we believe the asset will reach different points into the future.

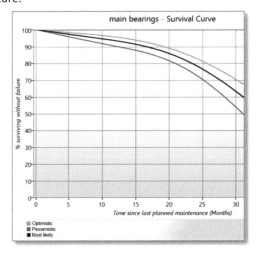

Figure 49. Survival Curve

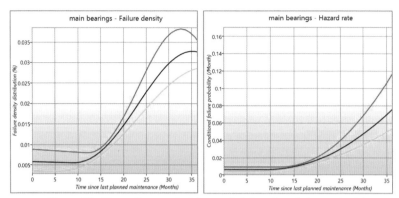

Figure 50. Converting survival forecasts into rates of change in risk

Complex mathematics are needed to convert our estimates of survival into the form needed for risk-based decision-making, but the DST software handles this with ease. The process involves calculating the gradient of the survival curve (the rate of change); this is the Failure Density Distribution or, in simple terms, how often the assets would have to fail at different time points for the survival curve to be true. The Failure Density is a distortion, however, because it is a product of both the failure risks and how many assets reach that point and are exposed to those risks. What we need is the Hazard Rate Curve – the risk that an asset faces *if it reaches each a particular time point*. This *conditional* probability of failure is what we must use for exploring different preventive maintenance strategies and intervals: it allows us to ask, for example "If we delayed the planned maintenance from 2 to 3 years, what would be the increase in probability of failure?".

Calculating the Hazard Rate involves dividing the Failure Density by the Survival Curve, to derive, for each point, the probability of failure for an asset that has survived so far. Figure 50 shows the Failure Density Distribution and Hazard Rates that correspond to the estimated Survival curve in Figure 49. Once we have the Hazard Rate (and estimates of failure costs and consequences), we can evaluate the risks associated with any preventive maintenance interval including, of course, a Run-to-Failure option (zero preventive maintenance).

5.4.4.3   Clock-resetting and Patch-and-Continue failures

The second important Reliability Engineering concept that we must understand is the different clock-resetting effects of corrective actions. This can have a big impact upon preventive maintenance strategies.   If the repair action, following an asset failure, achieves the same resulting condition as the PM task that we are evaluating, then the risk pattern has been reset and the next occurrence of the PM should be timed from this point.   If, on the other hand, the repair is a 'Patch-and-continue' activity, which does *not* achieve the same condition as the PM task would, then the subsequent risk of further failures, rate of degradation and urgency of next PM are largely unaffected.   So the next PM will occur at its normal interval since its last occurrence.

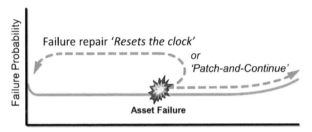

Figure 51. Clock-resetting and Patch-and-Continue failures

In between these two extremes, there are grey areas of 'partial restoration of condition' but in practice we usually find that the repair activity is of sufficient scope to achieve 'at least as good as PM' or is simply a localised, lesser task to recover functionality (Patch-and-Continue). There are also further complexities, known as 'Age-based' and 'Block-based' maintenance. 'Age-based' means that, following a Clock-resetting failure, the subsequent PM will be rescheduled from the date of the repair, whereas 'Block-based' maintenance means that, despite the Clock-resetting events, PM schedules remain locked to align with other activities.   These can also be explored and modelled but the probability of (multiple) failure implications get much more complicated very quickly.

5.4.4.4 Preventive maintenance example

The following is an example of a planned, periodic overhaul of the hydraulic roller assembly in a production environment. Similar analysis process is followed for any preventive maintenance activity.

Example: periodic overhaul of hydraulic roller assembly

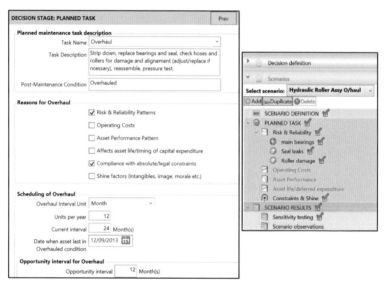

Figure 52. Configuration & storyboard for PM evaluation

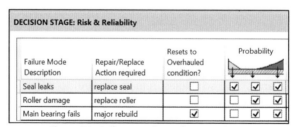

Figure 53. Failure modes to be considered

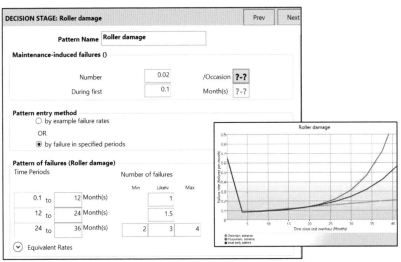

Figure 54. Pattern description for 'Patch-and-Continue' failure modes

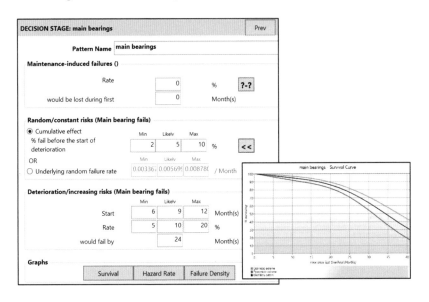

Figure 55. Pattern description for 'Clock-resetting' failure modes

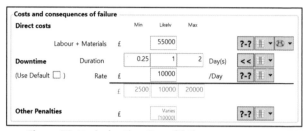

Figure 56. Typical estimation of failure consequences

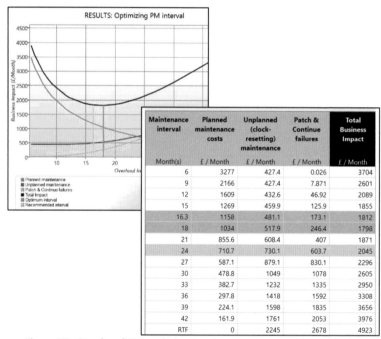

Maintenance interval	Planned maintenance costs	Unplanned (clock-resetting) maintenance	Patch & Continue failures	Total Business Impact
Month(s)	£ / Month	£ / Month	£ / Month	£ / Month
6	3277	427.4	0.026	3704
9	2166	427.4	7.871	2601
12	1609	432.6	46.92	2089
15	1269	459.9	125.9	1855
16.3	1158	481.1	173.1	1812
18	1034	517.9	246.4	1798
21	855.6	608.4	407	1871
24	710.7	730.1	603.7	2045
27	587.1	879.1	830.1	2296
30	478.8	1049	1078	2605
33	382.7	1232	1335	2950
36	297.8	1418	1592	3308
39	224.1	1598	1835	3656
42	161.9	1761	2053	3976
RTF	0	2245	2678	4923

Figure 57. Results of PM optimization showing Optimal interval (18), Recommended (16.3), current (24) and Run-to-failure (RTF) options

The optimal maintenance interval is 18 Month(s).
The recommended maintenance interval (taking data uncertainty into account) is 16.3 Month(s).
The potential impact of data uncertainty (if recommended interval is selected) is £302 /Month.
90% chance of asset survival to reach (selected) interval of 16.3 Month(s)

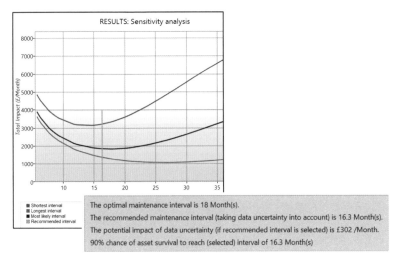

Figure 58. Sensitivity analysis and conclusions

Once the 'base case' strategy has been evaluated, alternative scenarios can be explored instantly; for example the potential impact of uprating the rollers and bearings (PM becomes more expensive but the reliability and survival patterns might be better). Figure 59 shows just one such comparison, revealing that the higher specification materials *are* worthwhile in this case, in terms of reduced Total (costs and risks) Impact.

Scenario	**Selected maintenance interval** Month(s)	**Optimal interval unconstrained** Month(s)	**Constrained interval** Month(s)	**Min-max range for optimum (uncertain data)** Month(s)	**TOTAL IMPACT for selected strategy** £ / Month
Current roller & bearing design	18	18	18	[15 - 27]	1800
Uprated rollers & bearings	24	21	21	[15 - 39]	1780

Figure 59. Evaluating alternative scenarios

5.4.4.5 Planned corrective maintenance

A very similar process is used to evaluate planned maintenance for recovering degraded performance. This is typical of progressively deteriorating asset efficiency, such as the fouling of heat exchangers, pumps, furnaces, boilers or piping. In such cases, there might be no clear-cut 'failure' point; just a slope of increasing energy costs or reducing asset or system performance. So the correct evaluation of maintenance timing involves determining how much deterioration we should tolerate before the corrective action (costs and, perhaps, downtime and/or introduced risks) becomes worthwhile.

This is a scenario in which many organisations make the mistake of short-termism in their decision-making, putting off the PM task as long as possible (especially if it will require downtime) instead of calculating the optimal mix of performance, costs and risks. Almost every single SALVO study of this type has revealed big tangible improvements compared to current practices.

Information needed to evaluate **planned maintenance to recover asset performance**:

- Direct and indirect (e.g. downtime) of the maintenance task; this is often variable or increases with maintenance interval as the degree of fouling or corrective work grows.
- Access opportunities and constraints (alignment with shutdowns and other activities).
- Failure risks introduced by the planned maintenance (e.g. human error).
- Pattern of asset performance losses following maintenance. This may be incurred as falling asset outputs (volumes, rates, quality etc.), or as increasing consumption of energy or materials to achieve a desired output. In some cases, both manifestations may be encountered – with rising operating costs *and* degrading outputs.
- Spare or buffer capacity to mitigate the losses and any 'biting point' after which performance losses start to have direct financial impact
- Value of the performance being affected, and its variability/uncertainty.

- Long term, cumulative effects of the periodic deterioration and corrective maintenance (e.g. shorter cleaning cycles may cause cumulative wear and shorten asset life).
- Compliance standards and absolute constraints on performance levels or maintenance frequencies.
- Shine factors associated with performance levels, quality and reputation etc.

Example: periodic cleaning of a heat exchanger

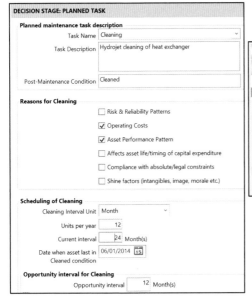

Figure 60. Configuration & storyboard for evaluating planned maintenance to recover performance

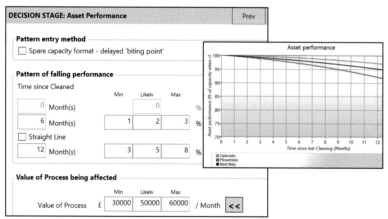

Figure 61. Quantifying patterns of falling performance

Calculating the financial impacts incurred under different maintenance strategies is a matter of quantifying the repeating areas under the curves of operating cost increases, or performance losses (see Figure 62). Of course the pattern of deterioration may not be regular, is unlikely to be linear and the value of the losses will often also be uncertain (hence the need for sensitivity testing and 'what if?' modelling).

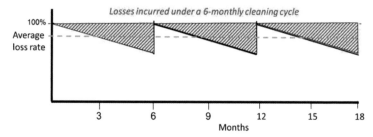

Figure 62. Example of losses resulting from cyclic cleaning

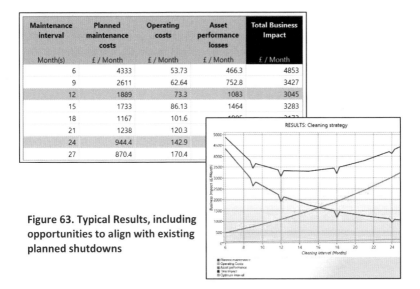

Maintenance interval	Planned maintenance costs	Operating costs	Asset performance losses	Total Business Impact
Month(s)	£ / Month	£ / Month	£ / Month	£ / Month
6	4333	53.73	466.3	4853
9	2611	62.64	752.8	3427
12	1889	73.3	1083	3045
15	1733	86.13	1464	3283
18	1167	101.6		
21	1238	120.3		
24	944.4	142.9		
27	870.4	170.4		

Figure 63. Typical Results, including opportunities to align with existing planned shutdowns

5.4.4.6   Maintenance to extend asset lifespan

The third family of evaluation methods for planned maintenance address the long term consequences of short term activities. In addition to the benefits of preventing asset failure, or recovering asset performance, planned maintenance can be targeted at *slowing down* the processes of deterioration.   The frequency of painting structural steelwork, for example, can influence the corrosion rate and ultimate replacement timing for the steel.   More painting in the short term might help to defer future   capital   expenditures   (as   well   as   delivering   Shine   benefits). Similarly, changing the oil in a gearbox reduces the wear rate and influences gearbox life. **Note**: this is a separate effect to the action of checking and topping up the oil level: an activity performed to reduce the risk of a 'lack of lubrication' failure mode.   *Checking* the oil is thus a risk-based preventive maintenance task, whereas *changing* oil regularly is a life-extending task.

The SALVO modelling methods for such effects are innovative and pragmatic, helping to range-estimate the degree of impact in the future, usually with little or no hard data to work with.   The modelling is also an example of interaction between planned activities on the same asset. The optimal strategy for managing the whole life cycle is a mix of the, for example, painting strategy and ultimate replacement strategy and, since they interact, we will need to consider the best value *combination*. This is called 'Blending' and is addressed more rigorously in Step 5 of the SALVO process. In the meantime, we will look at the evaluation of a discrete maintenance activity that influences asset lifespan or the future timing of some other large expenditure (such as major refurbishment).

Information needed to evaluate **planned maintenance that affects asset lifespan** or future major expenditure:

- Direct and indirect (e.g. downtime) of the maintenance task; this is often variable or increases with maintenance interval as, for example, the time and cost for preparation and painting escalates with time since last performed.
- Access opportunities and constraints (alignment with shutdowns and other activities).
- Failure risks introduced by the planned maintenance (e.g. human error).
- Boundary conditions for maximum achievable asset lifespan through adequate maintenance (i.e. at which some other consideration such as functional demand, obsolescence or other degradation mechanisms will become the life-limiting factor).
- Boundary conditions for minimum asset life obtained even if no maintenance is performed.
- Realistic example of a planned maintenance regime and the achievable life obtained.
- Capital value of the asset whose life is being affected (or the cost of the future activity, such as major refurbishment, that can be deferred by the maintenance).
- Discounting rate for future cashflows (also known as the 'cost of capital') – so that future deferments can be converted into present day financial significance.
- Preventive maintenance 'secondary' benefits through condition observation and defect elimination activity; these can sometimes be a big influence in the cost/benefit evaluation.
- Compliance standards and absolute obligations that apply to the maintenance activity.

- Shine factors associated with different maintenance intervals (often significant consideration for external painting).

Example: painting strategy for structural steelwork

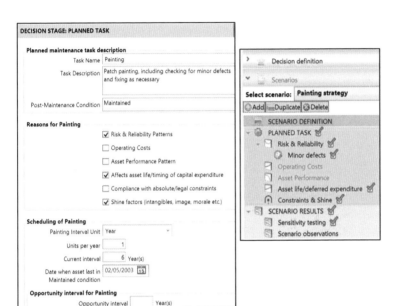

Figure 64. Configuration & storyboard for evaluating Maintenance to extend asset life

Quantifying the relationship between the (relatively) short cycle maintenance activity and the long cycle asset renewal or major expenditure is done by estimating the extreme cases and then calibrating or validating with a 'realistic estimate' to ensure that the interpolations are reasonable (see Figure 65). Note that the effects on asset life might be positive (life extension) or negative (if the maintenance cycle causes cumulative wear and damage).

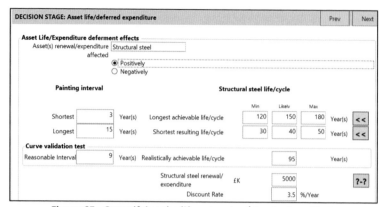

Figure 65. Quantifying the life extension/shortening effects

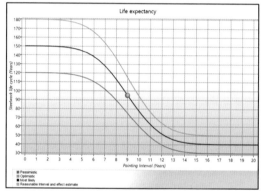

Figure 66. Interpolated relationship between extremes and validation checkpoint with 'reasonable estimate'.

Maintenance interval	Planned maintenance costs	Patch & Continue failures	Structural steel renewals/ expenditures	Total Business Impact
Year(s)	£K / Year	£K / Year	PV£K / Year	£K / Year
1	7	3.344	0.978	11.32
1.5	4.667	3.403	0.98	9.049
2	3.5	3.466	0.983	7.949
2.5	2.8	3.546	0.989	7.335
3	2.333	3.65	1	6.983
3.5	2.23	3.773	1.018	7.021
4	2.214	3.913	1.048	7.175
4.5	2.271	4.07	1.096	7.437
5	2.4	4.244	1.171	7.815
5.5	2.603	4.437	1.286	8.326
6	2.889	4.65	1.46	8.999
6.5	3.272	4.884	1.722	9.878
7	3.77	5.143		
7.5	4.408	5.428		
8	5.218	5.742		
8.5	6.243	6.09		
9	7.533	6.475		

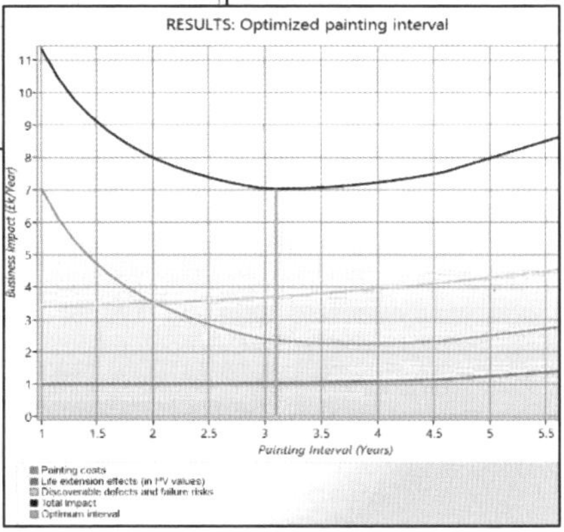

Figure 67. Results, showing Shine-preferred (purple), Optimum (green) and Current (pink) painting intervals.

In this case, the 'premium paid for Shine' (painting, for example, every 2 years instead of the financial optimum of 3-yearly) is calculated as just £k 0.966/year (difference in Total Business Impact between the purple and green lines in the Figure 67 table). Note also the annualized costs of painting decline initially as the painting interval extends, but then rise again as the cost-per-occasion grows (more preparation work is needed) and this impact is a significant reason for not painting at longer intervals.

5.4.5 Asset life cycle evaluations

Full life cycle costing is needed to evaluate several of the options identified in Step 3 of SALVO. New asset procurement, existing asset replacement and refurbishment require an evaluation of their whole life cycle impact. Similarly, decisions about any activities that might extend or shorten asset life also need to take a whole life view. So this area of Step 4 evaluation is extremely flexible and, potentially, complex if multiple options and scenarios are to be explored. It should be noted that changes during an asset's life (such as a change in operating regime or maintenance) will change the life cycle costs, and may also require re-evaluation of asset procurement or replacement implications. Figure 68 shows just a few of the permutations that can be modelled in asset renewal decisions.

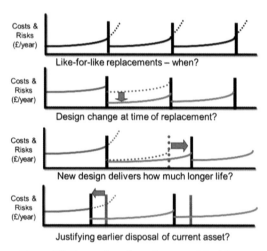

Figure 68. Examples of asset renewal decisions

The necessary life cycle modelling involves two primary Storyboards and a number of secondary variants:

1. **New asset procurements and option comparisons:** a 'greenfield' evaluation of the capital or investment costs, and the whole life profile of operating costs, risks, performance and sustainability impacts, including determining the optimum

lifespan before future replacement, and the fair comparison between design or procurement options (which may also have different lifespans).

2. **Existing asset replacements and/or life extensions**: the 'brownfield' evaluation of refurbishment and life extension options. This includes three variants that have significant effects on the 'storyboard' (i.e. what factors to consider and what calculations to perform):

   a. One-off refurbishments to extend life
   b. Like-for-like renewals and optimal timing
   c. Obsolescence and design changes at time of replacement (and optimal timing).

The SALVO process encourages us to consider the least intrusive, least cost options first before, if necessary, escalating to more substantive investments and interventions. So in life cycle cases, the first option to be considered is the extension of an existing asset life (rather than presume replacement is needed). However, for the purposes of this guidebook, it is easier to follow the process if we start with the simplest scenario – the life cycle cost evaluation of a new asset in a procurement decision.

5.4.5.1   Asset procurement (life cycle costing)

The ability to evaluate costs, risks and performance (i.e. total value) of an asset over its whole life cycle is a core skill for asset managers. Nevertheless, much confusion exists about how to evaluate the whole life cost, what to include, and what calculations are appropriate to represent future risks, cashflows and uncertainties. The SALVO process is highly pragmatic in this respect and assures the correct, selective use of appropriate techniques, such as the Net Present Value (NPV) and Equivalent Annual Cost (EAC), as decision-making criteria for options that have different horizons or life cycles.

The following is a list of information that may be useful in evaluating **whole life cycle costs**, risks, performance and sustainability:

- Procurement costs, including research, conceptual design, detailed design, purchase, construction, configuration, commissioning and any system downtime or indirect costs associated with commissioning.
- 'Infant-mortality' risks and commissioning problems, their likelihood, period of discovery, costs and consequences, and any warranty arrangements to recover such costs.
- Operating costs in all manifestations, including how these may change during the asset's life.
- Failure modes and effects; the profile of risks and failure modes, their probability patterns, costs and consequences.
- Corrective tasks for addressing failures including whether these are 'clock resetting events' or 'patch and continue'.
- Asset performance over the anticipated life, any deterioration pattern and financial impact of losses.
- End-of-life cashflows including resale, disposal, cost of decommissioning, and any residual risk liabilities.
- Depreciation rate in any recoverable value.
- Finite horizon constraints for asset utilisation (i.e. how long the asset will be required), functional demand, supply chain vulnerability (e.g. raw materials, spare parts, vendor support/obsolescence).
- Financial discounting rate and 'cost of capital' including inflation, interest rates and other effects upon investment (such as taxation impact).
- Compliance standards and absolute constraints on risks, performance or asset lifespan.
- Shine factors associated with asset design selection, performance, reliability, age or ongoing renewal strategy.

The evaluation Storyboard (Figure 68) is similar to that of Planned Maintenance (like-for-like asset renewal is a form of major periodic maintenance of the asset system). Some additional factors may have to be included, however, such as capital investment decision criteria (taxation and regulatory treatment etc.), and the use of discounted cashflow techniques to adjust future costs, risks and performance impacts to present day values.

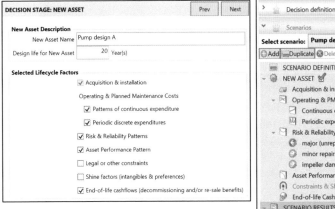
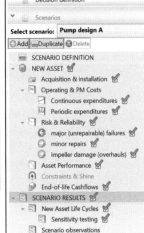

Figure 69. Configuration & storyboard for evaluating new asset by life cycle cost

The life cycle modelling uses the data entry processes, the risk quantification methods, the reliability engineering treatment of competing risks, and the range-estimating techniques introduced in the Planned Maintenance evaluation processes (section 5.4.4). Typical results also look similar – in this case demonstrating the optimal renewal cycle instead of maintenance interval (see figure 70). Another difference lies in the use of Equivalent Annual Cost (EAC) to adjust for the discounting of future expenditures and risks into present day values. This is the method that should be used to compare different life cycles and to compare asset design or procurement options if they have different usage horizons, performance patterns, risk profiles and ongoing renewal requirements. Net Present Value (NPV) calculations over a fixed planning horizon do not enable this, so NPV should only be used as a decision criterion with a horizon long enough to smooth out the differences between investment and re-investment cycles.

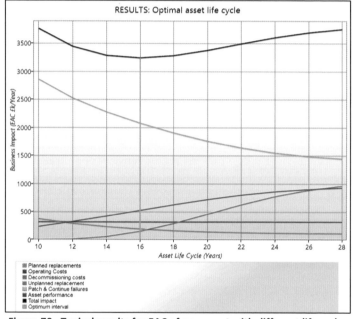

New asset life cycle	Planned replacement costs	Operating costs	End-of-life cashflows	Unplanned replacement costs	Patch & Continue costs	Asset performance	Total Impact (EAC)
Year(s)	£k / Year	£k / Year	£k / Year	£k / Year	£k / Year	£k / Year	£k / Year
10	2848	311	361.9	0	2.572	230.6	3754
12	2515	311	279.6	8.242	2.613	319.6	3436
14	2268	311.1	222.3	53.69	2.808	417.5	3275
16	2067	311.5	181.6	148.5	3.118	520	3232
18	1896	312.1	152.6	287.4	3.489	621.4	3273
20	1749	312.7	132.6	453.1	3.871	715.1	3367
22	1629	313.3	119.4	622.1	4.234	794.8	3483
24	1537	313.9	111.3	771.3	4.535	856.2	3594
26	1473	314.3	106.8	885.1	4.757	898.5	3682

Figure 70. Typical results for EAC of new asset with different life cycles

The big opportunity that this approach offers is the fair comparison between *dissimilar asset procurement options and/or life cycles*. The EAC measure of life cycle costs converts all cashflows, risks and performance impacts into an equivalent annualized rate (in present day values), so any complexity in future life cycles or different asset performance and risk patterns can be compared on fair basis. Scenario comparisons provide an easy and very rapid exploration of different designs, vendors, configurations, operating assumptions etc. (see figure 71). It should be noted that the annualized present value of future cost is for evaluation and comparison of options, and does not represent the actual cashflows for a particular year (for budgetary purposes, the undiscounted values need to be planned-for).

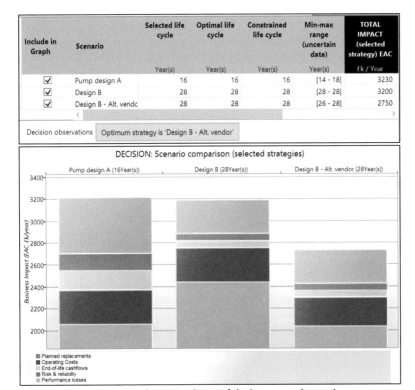

Include in Graph	Scenario	Selected life cycle	Optimal life cycle	Constrained life cycle	Min-max range (uncertain data)	TOTAL IMPACT (selected strategy) EAC
		Year(s)	Year(s)	Year(s)	Year(s)	£k / Year
☑	Pump design A	16	16	16	[14 - 18]	3230
☑	Design B	28	28	28	[28 - 28]	3200
☑	Design B - Alt. vendc	28	28	28	[26 - 28]	2750

Decision observations	Optimum strategy is 'Design B - Alt. vendor'

DECISION: Scenario comparison (selected strategies)

Planned replacements
Operating Costs
End-of-life cashflows
Risk & reliability
Performance losses

Figure 71. Scenario comparisons of design or vendor options

5.4.5.2   Existing assets: renewal justification and timing

The determination of optimal residual life of a currently-installed asset, is significantly more complex than the simple life cycle cost evaluation for procurement of a new asset. The correct evaluation involves quantifying the various predicted costs, risks and performance patterns into the future for both the existing asset (if not replaced) and the proposed replacement options. The complexity arises in the combined costs and risk exposures to a *'non-cyclic'* residual life of the existing asset and the procurement and ongoing *renewal cycles* of the new asset. The more attractive (lower total cost/risk) is the future asset life cycle cost, the sooner we will wish to replace the existing unit. Conversely, we may benefit financially by deferring the capital investment element of the replacement as long as possible, but will suffer from the existing asset's ongoing degradation and failure risks. Furthermore, the decision will be influenced by external factors such as new technology, obsolescence, supply chain vulnerabilities (e.g. to servicing expertise and spare parts), demand forecasts and system alignment considerations (such as standardisation and interchangeabilities).

SALVO provides great flexibility in the evaluation of existing asset renewals, ranging from simple like-for-like replacement justification and timing, to the scenario exploration of upgrades, spare parts scavenging and the different external constraints.

The base model for such decisions is a like-for-like renewal. SALVO enables improved asset replacement decisions, which can support a comprehensive and robust asset management strategy – leading to optimized cost/performance/risk and predictable (and justified) future capital requirements.

5.4.5.3 Like-for-like renewals

The Storyboard for a like-for-like renewal is organised as a 'before' and 'after' description of:

a) the ongoing costs, risks and performance of the current asset, and

b) the corresponding patterns for the new asset, suitably extended forwards to cover the initial acquisition and the whole life cycle (not just the end-of-life phase).

Figure 72 shows the Storyboard for replacing the lining of an ore crushing mill, where the only decision-critical factors included are the risks of lining failures and the degrading mill performance as the lining wears out. In other cases, the Storyboard may have any or all of the decision factors enabled and quantified as part of the evaluation.

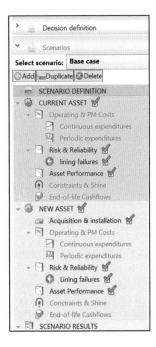

Figure 72. Storyboard for a like-for-like renewal decision

The calculations for this type of decision require a specific sequence of evaluations. Firstly the new asset life cycle cost needs to be calculated, including the determination of the optimal lifespan (if not constrained by other factors). This provides a total life cycle cost for the new asset, which can then be used as one of the inputs to the calculations of when to dispose of the current asset.

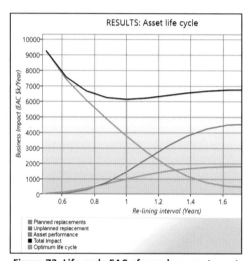

Figure 73. Life cycle EAC of a replacement asset

The new asset life cycle cost becomes one of the factors in the second stage of calculation – when to replace the current asset with the new one. Thus the overall strategy is a combination of selected new asset life cycles and residual life of the current asset. This 'total picture' approach is particularly useful when prioritizing short-term replacement projects while also building long-term asset management strategies.

Figure 74 shows the result, with the advantages of deferring the replacement (present value of ongoing life cycles of the new asset – purple line) traded against the costs, performance losses and risks of continuing with the current asset (red and orange lines). The big difference in vertical scales reflects the inclusion of capital costs within the new asset life cycles (the current asset is already paid-for, so only the costs, performance and risks of continued ownership need to be considered.

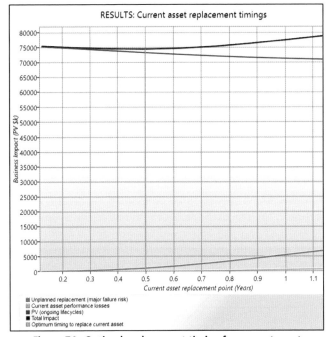

Figure 74. Optimal replacement timing for current asset

This example is a fairly short-horizon case (mill linings do not last long). However the same methodology has been widely used for capital investment and replacement decisions as diverse as petrochemical reactor vessels, underground pipelines, HV electric motors and transport vehicles. Because the discipline so often yields benefits compared to current, more subjective, methods for determining replacement timing, many of the SALVO Project participants now insist that <u>every</u> asset renewal decision must go through this process before it is even considered for management endorsement.

5.4.5.4 Obsolescence and design upgrades

The current rates of technology change and volatile commercial, energy, climate change and regulatory environments mean that asset renewal decisions often face significant constraints and opportunities in the options available. Technology obsolescence can impose a massive cost burden on an organisation – and the decisions about when to upgrade systems, or how to extend the useful economic life of the existing assets, are both hard and highly critical.

The SALVO evaluation process in such cases is similar to the like-for-like renewal decisions, but with explicit consideration of the changes introduced by the new asset. These can include elements of the procurement and installation that are non-repeating (i.e. not part of the ongoing life *cycles*), such as the reconfiguring of infrastructure and other one-off modifications needed to accommodate the asset change on the first occasion. The use of scenarios can then rapidly compare different procurement and upgrade options, to identify not just *when* to replace the current assets but also *with what*. The DST Lifespan Evaluator™ converts all the options into Total Business Impact, so they are directly comparable in net financial significance.

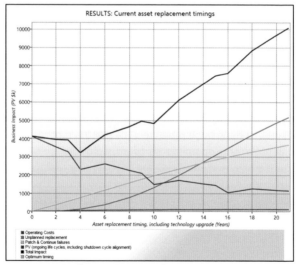

Figure 75. Optimal upgrade timing for 'obsolete' instrumentation, including alignment opportunities with site shutdowns.

EXAMPLE: Evaluating replacement of 'obsolete' control system

The instrumentation and control systems for 12 process plants of a multi-national oil company were installed the period 1977 to 1980, but came off the market in the mid-1980s. However spares, maintenance and support services have continued to be available until recently. Concerns about ongoing reliability, maintenance competencies and spares availability prompted a need to review replacement options and timings.

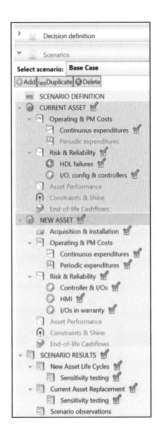

The resulting technical analysis proposed urgent replacement of all the unsupported obsolete equipment as soon as physically possible. The SALVO evaluation, however, demonstrated that, *even in the worst case scenario*, 2020-30 is the *earliest* period in which such a systematic replacement programme becomes worthwhile.

Using SALVO Step 3 to trigger lateral thinking and risk mitigation options, and Step 4 to evaluate and compare the different scenarios, a progressive, rolling replacement programme was developed, starting no sooner than 2020, and scavenging the spares from early replacements to extend the life even further for the less critical locations. The evaluation was done jointly with the vendor, and a new, 20-year support commitment was part of the resulting strategy.

The average life extension achieved for the existing assets was 10 years (compared to prior plans), generating a 60% total cost/risk saving in capital deferments, cost avoidance and risk reduction.

5.4.5.5 Existing assets: life extension options

Asset life extension can be achieved by changing the operating or maintenance regime, or by changing risk tolerance or mitigation options (e.g. holding spares, installing standby equipment or negotiating changes to stakeholder expectations). The examples covered in this guidebook are:

- Changes to operating environment, criticality and contingency plans. These are evaluated by scenario 'What if?' studies for their effect on asset life cycles (section 5.4.5.2). The evaluation of any capital investments that might be needed to achieve these changes can be performed with the Project/Change Evaluation process in section 5.4.2.
- Enhanced maintenance to slow down the rate of deterioration. This option is handled by the Planned Maintenance to Extend Asset Lifespan process covered in section 5.4.4.6.
- One-off refurbishment to restore condition and extend asset life. This is explained and illustrated below.

5.4.5.6 Evaluating refurbishment to extend asset life

SALVO uses the term 'refurbishment' specifically for one-off interventions that improve asset condition and extend asset life. The evaluation of such an intervention is another layer of complexity in the patterns of degradation, recovery and timings. In order to calculate the net effect of different options, such as refurbishment scope and timing, the degree of life extension and subsequent renewal options, a 3-stage storyboard is required (see Figures 76 and 77).

one-off refurbishment delivers how much longer life?

Figure 76. Modelling the effects of a one-off refurbishment

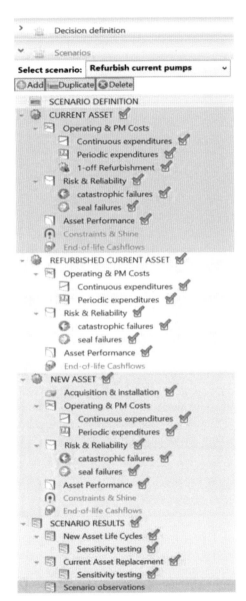

Figure 77. Storyboard for evaluating refurbishment to extend asset life (*including* subsequent replacement timing *and* future asset life cycles)

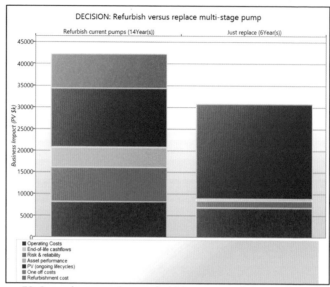

Figure 78. Scenario comparison: refurbish pumps and then replace after 14 years, or simply replace in 8 years (optimal timings in both cases).

5.4.6 Systematic reviews and batches of studies

When performing a series of studies within Step 4, such as the evaluation of a range of projects, or the optimization of maintenance activities, there are two programme management techniques that are particularly valuable:

a) Study prioritization criteria
b) Effective use of templates

These can be used in combination to great effect, reducing the overall analysis effort by up to 60%. To get it right, however, we need to consider the range of studies to be performed and the motive for their systematic evaluation.

5.4.6.1 Prioritizing the studies

Capital investment or engineering projects, for example, can vary widely in project type, size, leadtime to achievable benefits and degree of decision freedom (e.g. compliance obligations or discretionary timing). The prioritization criteria for their evaluation should, in the absence of any overriding consideration, be based on the greatest benefit opportunity and decision urgency. This will vary with circumstances but might represent, for example, the risks or 'lost opportunity costs' that are currently being suffered, the scope for deferring major expenditure if budget constraints mean that some jobs will no longer be affordable, or the speed/simplicity of performing the study - so decisions can be made, projects executed and benefits be obtained as soon as possible.

For *cyclic* activities there is a further consideration. If the assets are subject to a variety of inspection, maintenance and, ultimately, renewal strategies, then there is a sound reason for analysing the different activities in a particular order. SALVO guidance, in anticipation of Step 5 (blending and bundling of activities), requires us to evaluate and optimize the interval for the *shortest cycle activity first*, and, given the resulting optimized strategy, then consider the incremental reasons (other degradation mechanisms) and progressively longer-cycle interventions, up to and including the full asset replacement (life) cycle. This 'bottom up' approach to evaluating and optimizing different activities applied to the same asset(s) is explained in more detail in section 5.5.

5.4.6.2 Using templates effectively

The second 'tip' in managing a large number of evaluations efficiently is the development and usage of decision 'templates'. These are generic studies that have a high proportion of inputs common to the different cases that need to be evaluated, so that each individual case involves just editing the variables or factors that are case-specific, rather than creating a cost/benefit or optimization study from scratch each time.

There is a skill in selecting and creating the most valuable templates – both in terms of anticipating the shared data versus case-by-case customisations needed for the programme of studies being planned, and in establishing a useful library of such generic cases for future decision-making. In general, a template will be useful and effective if it represents a) a fairly common asset type and circumstance (e.g. functional role), and b) a fairly common intervention type (task and the reasons for it). Individual differences in either asset circumstances, or task cost/benefits, can then be made by adjusting the case-specific data items such as the likelihood and impact of failure, the condition or degradation rate or the access costs for the planned interventions.

A further finding of the SALVO Project was the importance of team engagement and sustained motivation in such programmes of study. The most time-efficient route to a large number of studies might be to select a common, 'average' case first, with the largest asset group size or widest applicability of the results, and also the greatest template value for ongoing usage in evaluating other cases. However, if team engagement in the process is a concern (for example, reluctant participants, or cynical attitudes resulting from experience of previous failed 'methodologies'), there can be a positive value of addressing an extreme case first. This typically demonstrates that the SALVO method can rapidly identify the optimal solution, and will often show very significant quantified $$ business benefits. It also reassures participants that their practical, tacit knowledge is represented appropriately in the agreed outcome. Once the attention-grabbing case is complete, the team is usually much more motivated to the systematic rollout to the larger volume of cases, including building a more typical case as the 'base case' template for the ongoing variants.

5.5   Step 5: Optimizing *combinations* of interventions

The next stage in the overall SALVO process is one of integration.   The evaluation of discrete interventions and options provides useful business justification for what is worth doing and when, but a second stage is needed in determining the best value *combination* of activities, particularly if the consequences of one activity influence the urgency, value or effectiveness of another.   Most assets will have a number of activities done to them during their lifespans, and there is a relationship between short cycle inspections, minor maintenance or servicing, and the longer timescale needs for more significant tasks (overhauls or even replacement).   If we do less minor maintenance, we may have to do more substantial maintenance later.   Step 5 of SALVO provides guidance in how to find the best mix of activities to deliver best whole life cycle value – this is called '**Blending**'. We have already encountered an example of this in the evaluation of Planned Maintenance to extend asset lifespan (see section 5.4.4.6).   This yielded the optimal combination of short cycle activity (e.g. painting) and longer cycle tasks (such as asset replacements). Step 5 of SALVO extends this capability to the generic process – how to build a systematic whole life cycle management strategy from a hierarchy of activities and competing priorities.

Step 5 also considers another form of coordination and combination of activities; in the optimization of work *delivery* programmes.   The evaluation of discrete interventions provided optimal timings for those tasks, and quantified the cost/risk impact of performing them too early or too late (the increases in Total Impact).   Step 4 evaluations could also consider alignment opportunities for the activities, for timings that exploited existing shutdowns (see example in section 5.4.5.4). However, Step 5 again converts this into the systematic approach – seeking the best coordination of multiple competing activities for potential shared downtime, access, resources, overhead costs and travel logistics.   In SALVO language this is called '**Bundling**'.

5.5.1 Blending of activities for best life cycle value

The evaluation of a single activity that has effects upon the need for another is handled in Step 4. The methods used to evaluate Planned Maintenance to extend asset life (such as painting or oil changes – see section 5.4.4.6) can equally be applied to any pair of interacting planned activities, provided we model the relationship between them for combined costs, risks, performance consequences etc. However, to do this for a full hierarchy of activities applied to an asset on different timescales, for different reasons (e.g. different degradation mechanisms), we must work from bottom upwards (Figure 79). The principle to remember is that longer timescale, more intrusive interventions are only needed because the shorter cycle activities do not fully address and control all the degradation mechanisms. If we optimise the shortest cycle activities first, then the need for further, longer cycle tasks is (correctly) based only on the longer term, cumulative degradation that the short-cycle tasks do not address. This is iterative – as we evaluate and optimize the timing of each bigger activity, *assuming the adoption of the previously optimized shorter cycle tasks*, we build a picture up to and including the optimal timing for total asset renewal (the ultimate maintenance activity).

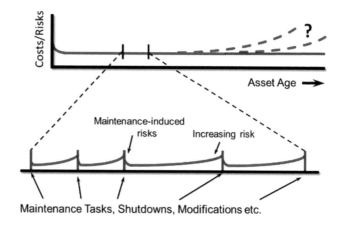

Figure 79. Interactions between risk patterns and asset interventions

---

Example: Switchgear maintenance strategy.

The conventional pattern for a certain type of HV switchgear was a combination of (mandatory) annual trip-tests and 3 yearly 'minor', 6 yearly 'intermediate' and 12 yearly 'major' maintenance packages.

By unbundling the work and evaluating the justification and optimal intervals for the individual tasks (taking just a few hours with the SALVO process), the optimal combination was found to be a change in scope and deferment of the 'minor' work to 4-yearly, combined with the most urgent elements of the former 'intermediate' work list, whose remaining scope was then deferred to join the 12-yearly 'major' (which was found to be about right in frequency).

So the 3, 6, 12 pattern was changed to a 4, 12 combination, with very significant reductions in costs, downtime and risks.

5.5.2   Optimal bundling of activities for delivery

The other form of Step 5 combinatorial studies is the seeking of delivery efficiencies through shared costs, downtime, resources or other overheads. This is particularly important in management of asset systems in continuous operation, where downtime is very costly. In such cases, there is a strong motivation to coordinate activities into intense planned shutdowns, 'turnarounds', 'outages' or 'possessions' (the names vary by industry sector). It is also commonly encountered in widely distributed asset networks, where remote site visits, with time and logistics costs, mean that opportunity alignment of activities can share such overheads.

The evaluation of optimal work bundling is therefore a case of quantifying the benefits obtainable by sharing costs, downtime or other overheads but also calculating the impact of performing the individual tasks at a sub-optimal timing – such as the additional risk created by waiting for the bundle opportunity, or a cost premium if the opportunity arises ahead of its personal optimum.   Seeking the best compromise among multiple activities, each of which has a cost/risk/performance trade-off involved, is a very complex task.   The SALVO research considered various technologies to assist in the 'combinatorial modelling' and found that conventional simulation methods could not cope with the volume and complexity – exploring just 10 activities over a 1-2 year planning horizon for their optimal timings and bundling (including alignments of tasks to every 2nd or 3rd occasion of others) represents 10^{27} possible permutations. This requires a simulation method known as Genetic Algorithms to explore the vast range of possibilities: as the name suggests, it exploits a random mutation and selective 'survival' process (Figure 80) to learn which activities work well in combination (alignment or at timing multiples of each other).   Performed tens of thousands of times, the search engine can filter out the poor alignments (high Total Impact EAC) and propose a good combined total programme (lowest Total Impact EAC).

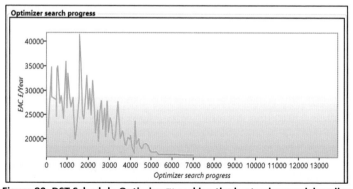

Figure 80. DST Schedule Optimizer™ seeking the best value work bundles

Before (each task performed at its 'personal' optimal timing)

Assembled (preferred)

Task Name	2013	2014	2015	2016	2017	2018	2019	2020	2021	2022	2023	2024	2025	2026
Pumps: Lifespan														
Control systems: Lifespan														
Electr system: test														

Schedule totals	2013	2014	2015	2016	2017	2018	2019	2020	2021	2022	2023	2024	2025	2026
Planned Capex	0	0	0	2150	0	15000	150	0	0	150	0	0	150	0
Planned Opex	1347	1347	1347	1347	1346	1346	1033	1033	1033	1033	1033	1033	1033	1033
Planned overhead	0	0	0	0										
Planned downtime impact	0	0	0	150000										0
Risk exposures	2343	2343	2343	2343	165									1386
Asset Performance losses	99.47	99.47	99.47	99.47	99.47	99.47	0	0	0	0	0	0	0	0
Other amortised costs	0	0	0	0	0	0	0	0	0	0	0	0	0	0
Total business impact	3789	3789	3789	155900	3101	68100	52570	2419	2419	52570	2419	2419	52570	2419

Total programme EAC £31,930/year

After (re-optimized for shared costs, downtime and overheads)

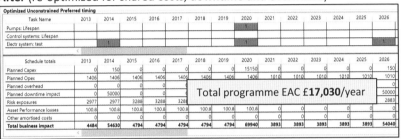

Optimized Unconstrained Preferred timing

Task Name	2013	2014	2015	2016	2017	2018	2019	2020	2021	2022	2023	2024	2025	2026
Pumps: Lifespan														
Control systems: Lifespan														
Electr system: test														

Schedule totals	2013	2014	2015	2016	2017	2018	2019	2020	2021	2022	2023	2024	2025	2026
Planned Capex	0	150	0	0	0	0	0	15150	0	0	0	0	0	150
Planned Opex	1406	1406	1406	1406	1406	1406	1406	1406	1010	1010	1010	1010	1010	1010
Planned overhead	0	0	0	0										
Planned downtime impact	0	50000	0	0										50000
Risk exposures	2977	2977	3288	3288	328									2883
Asset Performance losses	100.8	100.8	100.8	100.8	100.8	100.8	100.8	100.8	0	0	0	0	0	0
Other amortised costs	0	0	0	0	0	0	0	0	0	0	0	0	0	0
Total business impact	4484	54630	4794	4794	4794	4794	4794	69940	3893	3893	3893	3893	3893	54040

Total programme EAC £17,030/year

Figure 81. Effects of optimal bundling

The first systematic review in such a programme optimization often reveals one or more 'limiting factor' activities, which force a regular bundle to occur. These might be mandatory tests or inspections, or simply short cycle critical tasks with a big risk/consequence for being performed at longer intervals. So the SALVO methodology considers next how to eliminate the need for these tasks, or make whatever operational, asset or contingency planning changes (e.g. 'hot swapping' spares) as are necessary to 'de-bottleneck' the overall programme. Figure 81 shows the combined effect of such a process, yielding a 45% reduction in total programme costs/risks/downtime (EAC).

This process has now been applied to manufacturing plant shutdowns (reducing annual downtime by 50%), oil refineries (extending intervals between turnarounds by 2x) and outage planning for HV electrical transmission circuits (reducing planned downtime by 28%). In every case so far explored, the technique has re-mixed activities and timings, reduced total downtime, risks and costs to a remarkable degree – *with full transparency in what changes are worthwhile and why.*

EXAMPLE: shutdown strategy for process plant

Four plastics manufacturing plants in Europe and USA were each subject to a 2-yearly shutdown ('turnaround') cycle for inspections and maintenance. The study involved a criticality-filtered review of the c.7,800 tasks that potentially constrain shutdown intervals in each business unit, followed by the SALVO Step 4 evaluation of the individual task urgencies and optimal intervals. The Step 5 optimal bundling then revealed scope for moving to a 4-year cycle if only a few small plant changes (minor modifications and purchase of some 'hot swap' spare equipment) were implemented.

All these changes were approved and implemented within 24 months, and all plants now run for 4 years between major shutdowns. The total study in each site, took a small multi-disciplined team just eight weeks to filter the tasks and evaluate all the timing-sensitive inspections, maintenance tasks, projects and asset renewals. The net cost/risk/performance impact of the changed strategy was worth **US$7-digit annual business benefits to each site.**

5.6 Step 6: Assemble total portfolio & programme

The final SALVO step is one of aggregation and re-grouping of the implications of all that needs to be done. This is an assembly of all the tasks that have been justified, either individually or collectively, blended and/or bundled, into a total picture of activities, costs, risks and performance implications into the future. Step 6 provides the consolidated budgets for capital investments, for operating costs and for resource planning (Figure 82).

Assembled (preferred) Task Name	2014	2015	2016	2017	2018	2019	2020	2021	2022	2023	2024
Pumps: Lifespan											
Car: Lifespan	0										
Equipment: Lifespan	0	0	0	0	0	0	0	0	0	0	0
Control systems: Lifespan				0							
Heat Exchangers: Maintenance	0	0	0	0	0	0	0	0	0	0	0
Production line: Overhaul	0	0	0	0	0	0	0	0	0	0	0
structures: Painting		0			0			0			0
Pipeworks: Measurement								0			
Electr system: test						1	1	1	1	1	1
Primary compressor: Project	1										
Cooling fans: Project	0										
Heat Exchangers: Project	0										

Planned totals	2014	2015	2016	2017	2018	2019	2020	2021	2022	2023	2024
Planned Capex	2634000	166700	166400	168400	166400	181500	166500	166800	166500	166500	1665
Planned Opex	5455	4423	4417	4417	4415	4415	4072	4072	4072	4072	40
Planned downtime impact	0	0	0	0	0	2	2	2	2	2	
Risk exposures	3116	3993	3987	3987	3785	3785	2733	2733	2669	2669	26
Asset Performance losses	2047	2108	2108	2108	2108	2108	2009	2009	2009	2009	20
Other amortised costs	4	4	4	4	4	4	4	4	4	4	
Total business impact	2645000	177200	176900	178900	176700	191800	175300	175600	175300	175300	1753

Figure 82. Consolidated programme with costs, risks and resources

This is the material that senior executives often want to see and to understand: what is the optimal expenditure profile, and with what risk, performance and other consequences? Emerging from the SALVO 'Smiley', the information has full drill-down evidence supporting it, fully quantified, including the levels of uncertainty, the alternatives that are possible, and the impact of sub-optimal timing (e.g. the effects of not doing any task, or deferring it).

Individual activities or bundled tasks can also be 'shuffled' forwards or backwards to explore the combined cost/risk and sustainability impact, displayed in real time. So short term constraints can be converted directly into longer term financial and risk implications, quantified in present day values. Similarly, the effects of Shine can be explored across the activity programme, by calculating, instantly, the net premium paid for acceleration or promotion of specific activities to satisfy particular stakeholder expectations.

Global 'what if?' studies can also be applied at this level, such as the exploration of resource constraints or limited budgets (see Figure 83, drawing directly on the individual project cost/benefit/risk criteria from Step 4).

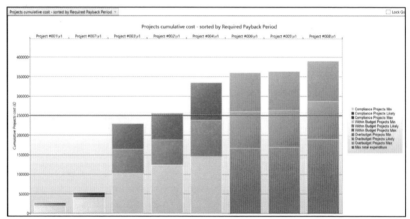

Figure 83. Ranked projects within a constrained capital budget
blue = mandatory, green = best value, red = not affordable

5.6.1   Feedback loops and continual improvement

Step 6 can also be a starting point in the SALVO process: sometimes it is stage at which problems are identified in the first place. If budgets are squeezed, or total resource implications found to be undeliverable, then the alarm may be raised and a systematic review initiated (SALVO Step 1), discrete problems investigated (Step 2), or specific intervention changes or alternatives evaluated (Step 4).   So the SALVO Smiley is really a continual improvement process, with feedback loops and iterations within each step and between steps. However it provides an important underlying pattern of 'top-down' problem investigation and 'bottom-up' justification of what to do, when and why.

6 Conclusions

The SALVO process has brought together a number of vital threads. It has addressed the core human factors involved in decision-making (motivation, conflicting agenda, cross-disciplinary collaboration and methods of capturing and quantifying 'tacit' knowledge). It provides a process rigour to ensure that the right questions get asked, of the right people, in the right way, and that the information is used correctly. These processes incorporate a number of existing good practices and common sense, in some cases with care and selective application to compensate for their limitations. And SALVO has also made a number of technology innovations in the 'what if?' evaluation of different options through very rapid and advanced mathematics and modelling.

These methods must be seen as an integrated whole – not just the application of some decision support tools, or the change in business processes. They require a planned combination of education, process introduction and enabling tools, with the leadership understanding of what is involved, and the engagement of the workforce (both as important sources of knowledge and as implementers of the decisions). Fortunately the transparent nature of these methods and the ability to handle uncertain information greatly improves acceptance and support when the techniques are introduced. Nevertheless, it is important to plan the introduction of such methods carefully, building on local case studies to establish credibility and 'ownership' of the methods. The detailed SALVO Technical Playbook provides extensive guidance, templates and practical tips in this respect, including the cross-disciplinary teamworking processes, facilitation expertise and interfaces to existing information systems and business processes.

Overall, the SALVO methods have proved to be highly flexible and understandable by those needing to make asset management decisions and the stakeholders they seek to satisfy. Most importantly of all, they have consistently revealed very big benefits compared to current normal decision-making methods.

John Woodhouse, SALVO Programme Director, 2009-2013

About the author

John Woodhouse is one of the most widely known experts in integrated asset management. He is a Founder, Fellow and Chair of the Panel of Experts for the Institute of Asset Management (IAM). He Chaired the BSI/IAM development of the PAS 55 standard for optimal management of physical assets, and was UK Expert Representative in the development of the first International Standard for Asset Management (ISO 55000).

He has also led the development of the first published Asset Management Competences Framework (IAM 2006), and was Programme Director for the European MACRO Project (EU1488) and International SALVO consortium, researching and developing best practices in asset management decision-making and in optimization of life cycle value.

John is CEO of the consulting and training organization, TWPL, providing advice and competency development to most industry sectors in over 25 countries. With a personal background as a senior manager in the oil industry (mix of oil and gas production and downstream/refining) and engineering (with Kvaerner Engineering UK), he launched TWPL in 1995 with a group of former senior industrial managers from nuclear, oil, utilities, defence and manufacturing sectors. 20 years on TWPL is one of the most experienced international sources of pragmatic advice and implementation support to organisations wishing to improve their asset management.

John holds a Masters degree from the University of Cambridge, where he was also captain of the varsity Boat Race crew. He has also skippered a round-the-world sailing yacht and is author of the book *'Managing Industrial Risk'* (Publ. Chapman & Hall, 1993). He now lecturers widely around the world at conferences and through university and in-house management training programmes.